Lifting the
Shadow of War

Pierre Elliott Trudeau
Lifting the Shadow of War

C. David Crenna,
EDITOR

Hurtig Publishers Ltd

Edmonton

Hurtig Publishers Ltd.
10560–105 St
Edmonton, Alberta
Canada T5H 2W7

Canadian Cataloguing in Publication Data

Trudeau, Pierre Elliott, 1919–
   Pierre Elliott: lifting the shadow of war

   ISBN 0-88830-300-9
   1. Trudeau, Pierre Elliott, 1919–
   Views on international relations.   2. World politics —
   1975–1985.   3. Arms race.   4. International relations.
   5. Great powers
   I. Crenna, C. David.   II. Title.   III. Title: Lifting
   the shadow of war

   D849.T78 1986   327.1′1′0924   C86-091289-2

Editor: Jean Wilson
Design: Jack Steiner Graphic Design
Composition: Attic Typesetting Inc.
Manufacturer: John Deyell Company

Edited, designed, typeset, printed, and bound in Canada

To Olof Palme, former Prime Minister of Sweden, cut down by an assassin on February 28, 1986

Contents

Foreword

*I*n these pages, you will find the written record of my views as Prime Minister of Canada, and more recently in retirement on the issue of peace and security. It obviously does not constitute a memoir, but it may recall some themes I tried to advance as the leader of a middlepower, as well as the specific actions my Government took.

While circumstances, personalities, and some trends have changed, certain major elements of these ideas remain, I think, quite relevant to today's conditions. This is not so much because I have been prescient, as because fundamental relationships between East and West and among nations in certain regions remain as complex and as filled with peril as ever.

The People's Republic of China has been brought fully into the community of nations, so my concerns about it as a potential threat to security appear dated. Many crises which threatened world peace have arisen and receded. However, there are at any one time a dozen "little wars" under way on the face of the globe, none of which is small in the suffering and loss caused.

The leaders of both superpowers have indicated a belief that a nuclear war cannot be won, and must never be fought. The strength of their commitment to this belief has yet to be demonstrated in a sustained mutual reduction in current stockpiles of instruments of nuclear doom. We live in hope mingled with scepticism.

Old prose may not leap out at you from the page. I hope, however, that this book will prove a useful reference for scholars, a source for students of recent Canadian history, and perhaps another stimulus for those active in the field to carry on and help achieve more.

PIERRE ELLIOTT TRUDEAU

A SINGULAR VOICE:
THE FOREIGN POLICY OF
PIERRE ELLIOTT TRUDEAU

THOMAS S. AXWORTHY

Throughout history, mankind has thought about foreign policy in two distinct ways.[1] Grounded in differing assessments of human nature, both philosophies descend from a long intellectual tradition. Each tells us part of the truth about ourselves.

The first approach originates with the ancient Greeks. Best expressed by Thucydides, this tradition of power politics or realism, to use the name most favoured by its practitioners, starts with the proposition that man perpetually pursues his interests defined in terms of power. Because anarchy is the condition, security is the objective, power is the means, and military force is the instrument. Only a balance of power can prevent war in this primitive state of nature. "The strong do what they can," Thucydides writes, "the weak do what they must."[2]

Contending with the view that man is inherently aggressive, that power is the only objective worth pursuing, and that mortality cannot be applied to the savage world of international politics is the approach called liberal idealism. Originating with the Christian fathers, gaining momentum with Grotius's first formulation of international law, and finding its fullest intellectual expression in Immanuel Kant's *Perpetual Peace* (1795), this view holds that mankind forms a community, that even princes should be subordinate to the rule of law, and that reason must govern the use of armed might.

Since the apogee of Woodrow Wilson, liberal foreign policy has been in slow, painful retreat. It was once the dominant school in Anglo-American practice, but the twentieth century has not been kind to the followers of Cobden, Bright, Gladstone, Bryan, and Roosevelt. Nazism, Stalinism, and modern terrorism offer horrifying evidence of the depths of mankind's depravity. Two world wars undermined belief in the efficacy of international law. Hopes for a new world order have dimmed as the United Nations General Assembly has talked itself into near irrelevancy. Moral values have given way to calculations of material advantage. Nuclear weapons threaten the future of humanity. We live in an age of fear rather than faith.

THE REALIST CONSENSUS

One result of this malodorous record has been the rise of a stunning orthodoxy in the field of international relations. Practitioner and theorist alike share the same precepts. Statecraft and scholarship have moved as one. Realism is now the established religion of the state and of the university. We speak only the language of power and interest, the "froids monstres," in de Gaulle's phrase, of the realist tradition.[3]

Three prominent scholars — Reinhold Niebuhr, Hans J. Morgenthau, and George F. Kennan — made the intellectual case for realism.[4] Sober, prudent, and pessimistic, these men were the opposite of military adventurers and each of them opposed American involvement in Vietnam. Realism does not necessarily imply an automatic resort to force.

Niebuhr, one of the twentieth-century's most prominent theologians, was a

Christian pessimist. "The children of darkness," he writes, "are evil but wise because they understand the power of self-interest. The children of light are virtuous but foolish because they underestimate the peril of anarchy in both the national and international community."[5] Morgenthau, author of the most widely read text in international relations theory, *Politics among Nations*, made explicit the realist fascination with power. "Whatever the ultimate aims of international politics," he generalizes, "power is always the immediate aim."[6] Kennan, the father of Soviet "containment," questions the liberal assumption that state behaviour is a fit subject for moral judgement. The most serious fault of American diplomacy, he maintains, is "the legalistic–moralistic approach to international problems."[7]

The intellectual arguments of Niebuhr, Morganthau, and Kennan against the tenets of liberal idealism ran in tandem with the tides of history. The Cold War converted even the most idealistic to realism. For a few brief months after World War II the high hopes of Franklin Roosevelt for a new international order hung in the balance, but the Cold War reduced the world to two armed camps. American liberalism became traumatized by the fear of being seen as too soft on communism. Progressives in other Western nations also joined the realist consensus.

Michael Howard notes with some irony that despite having Ministers like Sir Stafford Cripps and Philip Noel-Baker, who had made their reputations as tireless advocates of disarmament, it was the Labour government of Clement Attlee that took the decision to make Great Britain into a nuclear power.[8]

The individual who has best personified the contemporary realist consensus is Henry Kissinger. Both as a scholar and as a practitioner Kissinger has promoted a realist world view. The United States, he proclaimed in an essay published just before he became National Security Advisor to Richard Nixon, must think "in terms of power and equilibrium."[9] Kissinger's overriding goal was to found American foreign policy on a sober perception of permanent national interest. He believed in a concert of powers whose mutual interest in stability overrode their fundamental antagonisms. "If history teaches anything," he wrote, "it is that there can be no peace without equilibrium and no justice without restraint."[10]

Except as a locale for superpower rivalry, the Third World was not an important part of the Kissinger universe. Transnational issues, like the movement of international capital, were a nuisance. Backstairs diplomacy, secret operations to destabilize a regime in Chile, and even a clandestine war in Cambodia were all acceptable instruments of policy as long as they led to the emergence of a stable order. Coherent as his policies were in practice, they have become even more elegant in retrospect. Kissinger's memoirs were almost a primer in the precepts of realpolitik. To the realist Bible, Kissinger has added a new gospel.

THE TRUDEAU DISSENT

Few strayed from the postwar realist orthodoxy. One contrarian appeared in Canada. Pierre Elliott Trudeau began his career as an intellectual who read widely — Acton, Newman, Mounier, and Maritain — and formed clear views on the nation-state. He ended it with a peace mission worthy of Gladstone. For sixteen years, as Prime Minister of Canada, Trudeau consistently promoted a liberal world view at odds with the assumptions and practices of realist foreign policy.

The speeches, statements, and documents in this book can be read as a single man's public record. They represent the views of a liberal in power during a conservative age, of a man who had to make compromises and learn to take the world as it is. The passionate Professor Trudeau of 1963 attacking the decision of Lester B. Pearson to accept nuclear weapons was a different man from the Prime Minister twenty years later who reluctantly conceded the need to test Cruise missiles over the Canadian North. But as de Gaulle said in contrasting intellectuals with men in power, it is the statesman who takes risks, including moral ones.[11]

Values matter. The perceptual map that each of us brings to a subject highlights certain factors, ignores others, and aids us in finding causal connections. Pierre Trudeau's love of liberalism — his commitment to reason, individualism, and sharing — led him down a different path from Henry Kissinger's attachment to scepticism, power, and order.

Such a contrast, however, should not be drawn too sharply. There are few absolutes in politics and fewer still in foreign policy. Trudeau understood realism, shared some of its assumptions, and was as hard-headed as they come in assessing risks and probabilities. He had read widely in liberal philosophy but he had immersed himself equally deeply in modern European history. His recall of specific elements in Napoleon's various military campaigns, for example, was uncanny. This was a man who understood well the European tradition of balance of power. And his acceptance of great-power spheres of influence often got him into trouble with Canadians, who demanded a more forthright condemnation of either Soviet actions in Poland or American activities in Central America.

But despite his tough demeanour and ready use of realism's vocabulary in describing the national interest, at his core, Pierre Trudeau was a liberal idealist. He fitted Kant's description of a moral politician: "one who so interprets the principles of political prudence that they can be coherent with morality."[12]

The man who came to power questioning the Pearsonian tradition of Canada the "helpful fixer" left office after a world-wide crusade for peace. Prudence, of course, often dictated compromise with principle, as in the case of testing the Cruise missile to fulfil alliance obligations. Realism asked that the world be accepted for what it is; liberalism demanded that we try to transform it. Despite the frustrations and disappointments, Trudeau never stopped trying.

THE LIBERAL CRITIQUE

In word and deed, Trudeau took issue with three central propositions of realism. The first is that the state is the centre of the international system. Machiavelli put it best when he elevated the purpose of the state above all other moral considerations and made defence of one's country the critical objective of international politics.

> For where the very safety of the country depends upon the resolution to be taken, no considerations of justice or injustice, humanity or cruelty, nor of glory or shame should be allowed to prevail. But putting all other considerations aside, the only question should be, what course will save the life and liberty of the country?[13]

Trudeau's starting-point, however, was not country but community. Expressed most eloquently in his Mansion House speech, Trudeau's emphasis was always on the interdependence of the planet. Whatever the particular topic — arms control, economic development, or environmental protection — Trudeau asserted that "we are all brothers."

Paeans to world community are the staple fare of most addresses to the United Nations; but for Pierre Trudeau, planetary interdependence was the real reality, state sovereignty the artificial construct. In this belief, he was probably unique among world leaders. However they have clothed their actions in benign words about international community, most leaders fight like demons for national advantage. However hard he fought for policies favouring Canada's national advantage, Trudeau insisted on knowing how they would lead to global improvement. This distinction was not mere sophistry. Flag-waving patriotism was simply alien to his being. Pierre Trudeau, while Prime Minister of Canada, was really a citizen of the world. To the fundamental question of who is our neighbour he had only this answer: "we are one on this earth."

Power is the second preoccupation of realism, but Trudeau insists on a prior value — justice. No statesman, of course, can be oblivious to the benefits of a balance of power. It underlines the logic of our whole system of nuclear deterrence which Trudeau, along with others, fought to preserve from destabilizing concepts like the Strategic Defence Initiative. The need for countervailing power and the quest for equilibrium equally animate the Trudeau view of federalism.

But as Stanley Hoffman reminds us, order must have a context beyond equilibrium: otherwise it becomes pure mechanics.[14] Trudeau recognized that security is not an end in itself. It is only a setting that permits man to pursue primary values like freedom, artistic expression, and the fulfilment of the human personality. To attain these ends, we need not only a safe world but a just one.

Trudeau's analysis of international security therefore returned again and again to moral questions of distributive justice. For Trudeau, sharing abroad was like sharing at home, part of the moral fabric. His extensive travels as a student had widened his definition of world community. His membership in a francophone minority at home sensitized him to the plight of the powerless.

If the state is the primary locus of action and power the goal, for realists, military force is the central way to gain power. A modern realist like Kissinger rarely discusses even economics: for him the military equation is the principal concern. In a world where over 130 wars have been fought since 1945, no one can deny that armed force is still at the heart of the international system. But liberals insist that other sources of influence also have a place.

Trudeau is not a pacifist, but critics fault him for neglecting the Canadian military. There is no need to be defensive about this record.

In 1980, true to conservative values, Ronald Reagan cut social and economic programs in his country to boost the American armed forces. In 1969, true to liberal values, Pierre Trudeau made a choice in favour of health and social security over an expanded budget for the Department of National Defence. The bills for Lester Pearson's welfare state, especially for medicare, arrived just as Pierre Trudeau assumed office. Choices had to be made. Was it to be improved care for an aging population or improved sonar for aging destroyers? No doubt it would have been nice to fund defence *and* health, but it was not a perfect world. Values dictated both the choices of Trudeau and

Reagan. Philosophies mattered. And so did external events. When détente began to fade in 1975 Canada became one of the few NATO nations to achieve the alliance target of a 3 percent real increase in military spending.

If Pierre Trudeau refused to buy power through a blank cheque for the military, did that mean that Canadian foreign policy was without influence, as realists would predict? Any fair assessment would conclude that, in the Trudeau era, Canada developed multiple channels of influence. By way of example and declaration, Trudeau scrapped Canada's reliance on nuclear weapons and created a nuclear-free military. Through increased aid, trade, and sensitive diplomacy, Canada expanded its role in the Commonwealth and La Francophonie. Canadian legal expertise and scientific capacities were displayed to good effect on issues like the law of the sea, nuclear proliferation, and the environment.

Canada's economic strength won us a seat at the Economic Summit. In the last great initiative of his career, Prime Minister Trudeau used the tactic of public diplomacy in an attempt to inject political will into a deteriorating superpower relationship.

So while still important, military strength is no longer the sole foundation of a foreign policy. Creative leaders can use reason, public opinion, technical expertise, economic muscle, and international organizations to achieve their ends. The career of Pierre Trudeau has demonstrated that, in a complicated world, multiple objectives require multiple instruments. Trudeau carried out an activist foreign policy without the burden of an excessive military budget. Here, too, there are lessons to be learned.

Yet the Trudeau record was not without its blemishes. Foreign aid was increased but the amount never matched the soaring rhetoric of the Prime Minister. A NATO review was launched in 1969; by the early 1980s, one was needed even more because of NATO's doctrine of early first use of nuclear weapons; but the government contented itself with private criticism rather than public debate. Most disappointing of all was the sad history of Trudeau's Third Option. Seldom has a policy been more apropos. Instead of hitching our destiny to a declining American hegemony, Trudeau sought to expand our links with Asia and Europe. We would be a player on the world stage, not just North America. The policy failed because of lack of will. The Ottawa mandarinate, especially in Finance, hoped that the policy would go away, and eventually it did. Unlike the repatriation of the Constitution or the National Energy Program, where Trudeau's personal drive forced a reluctant system to move, his commitment to the Third Option was not equal to the task. With the 1976 election of the Parti Québécois, Trudeau chose to husband his resources for the domestic showdown. This was understandable but regrettable. Because his attention was directed elsewhere, the Third Option died a silent death.

THE WAY AHEAD

Pierre Trudeau may have emphasized world community, justice, and reason instead of national interest, power, and military security, but his is a minority view. Realism still dominates the foreign policy perspective of most Western leaders. Compared to the sophistication of a Kissinger or a Kennan, Reagan-style realism is more like a California mutant; but most of the essential elements of the realist faith remain: in Washington today there is a single-minded determination to pursue the American national interest; little attention is paid to collective initiatives like the law of the sea; military power is foremost, with a trillion dollar defence build-up; conventional norms of morality are flaunted with the Contra War to overturn the Sandanista revolution.

Cracks, however, are appearing in the foundations of realist orthodoxy. The vast arms build-up has not noticeably improved the West's security. The illogic of piling nuclear weapon upon nuclear weapon, so that there are now 50,000 nuclear warheads poised at the ready, has been recognized by American and Soviet leaders. Both are under increasing pressure to strike an arms control deal. Democracy has won stunning victories in Latin America and the Philippines, showing once again how much the world yearns to be free. The terrible dilemma of South Africa daily assaults Western public opinion. Starvation in the sub-Sahara demonstrates anew that the world cannot long continue to ignore the disparity between rich and poor. Despite the dominance of the realists, moral issues are far from dead.

The liberal agenda today is the same as in the heavenly city of St. Augustine. Values must supercede power. Collective gains are more important than national advantage. Arms must be controlled. Understanding must be increased. Disparities must be reduced. Slowly, ever so slowly, the international law of the jungle must evolve into a civilized society. Pierre Trudeau has helped work toward this in his time. We must do the same in ours.

NOTES

1 I am grateful to Geoffrey Pearson, Janice Stein, De Montigny Marchand, Stephen Clarkson, John Kirton, John Roberts, and Michael Gillan for helpful remarks about earlier versions of this essay.

2 The Melian Debate captures in a few phrases enduring insights into the central problem of ethics and power politics. See Thucydides, *History of the Peloponnesian War*, translated by Rex Warner (Harmondsworth, Middlesex: Penguin Books Ltd., 1966), especially Book Five, Chapter 7, pp. 358-66.

3 Quoted in Michael Howard, *The Causes of War* (Cambridge, MA: Harvard University Press, 1984), p. 229.

4 See Reinhold Niebuhr, *Moral Man and Immoral Society* (New York: Charles Scribner's Sons, 1932); George F. Kennan, *American Diplomacy 1900-1950* (Chicago: University of Chicago Press, 1951); and Hans J. Morganthau, *Politics among Nations*, 4th ed. (New York: Alfred A. Knopf, 1966).

5 Reinhold Niebuhr, *The Essential Reinhold Niebuhr: Selected Essays and Addresses*, Ed. Robert McAfee Brown (New Haven: Yale University Press, 1986), p. 166.

6 Morganthau, *Power among Nations*, p. 25.

7 Kennan, *American Diplomacy*, p. 82.

8 Howard, *The Causes of War*, p. 55.

9 Henry A. Kissinger, *American Foreign Policy* (New York: W.W. Norton and Co. Inc., 1969), p. 92.

10 Henry Kissinger, *White House Years* (Boston: Little, Brown and Company, 1979), p. 55. See also his *Years of Upheaval* (Boston: Little, Brown and Company, 1982).

11 Quoted in Stanley Hoffmann, *Duties beyond Borders: On the Limits and Possibilities of Ethical International Politics* (Syracuse, NY: Syracuse University Press, 1981), p. 18.

12 Immanuel Kant, *Perpetual Peace and Other Essays*, translated by Ted Humphrey (Indianapolis, IN: Hackett Publishing Co., 1983), p. 128.

13 Niccolò Machiavelli, *The Prince and the Discourses* (New York: Modern Library, 1950), p. 528.

14 See Hoffman, *Duties beyond Borders*, pp. 141-87, for an excellent discussion of the issue of distributive justice and foreign policy.

Introduction

*P*oised somewhere in mid-air between archivist, historian, and journalist, the editor of a book of documents from the recent past has many choices. Because of the substantial and continuing public interest in the life and works of Pierre Elliott Trudeau, I have opted for readability over purist scholarship.

The former Prime Minister's complete and unedited statements on peace and security, as on other issues, are to be found in the Public Archives of Canada, which has a conscientious and interested staff. Many have been collected in an accessible form by the Department of External Affairs as well, and these are listed in the bibliography.

In this book, you will find the texts of his key statements on defence, conflict resolution, arms control, and disarmament. I have edited them to remove dated references and to avoid repetition of essentially the same material. Mr. Trudeau devoted considerable time to reviewing the draft text in detail and provided many helpful comments. However, the editorial choices which have been made throughout are my responsibility alone.

Grouped with the major statements, as relevant, are excerpts from other documents. These include transcripts of press conferences and interviews which help to illuminate further Mr. Trudeau's main ideas and their practical implications. Also included, but with "Document" as a heading, are certain essential documents and statements in which Mr. Trudeau had a significant hand, but which are not *his*, per se.

One of my most difficult choices as an editor was whether to stick to a chronological presentation or to select major subjects and build on them, regardless of chronology. This book groups speeches and documents according to larger themes, but retains chronological order throughout. By design or accident, the two methods of organization do not diverge.

Prime Minister Trudeau's major speeches on peace and security were often drafted by others, either on his own staff or in the Department of External Affairs. This is true for all government leaders, and for many busy executives. This does *not* mean, however, that they were not *his* speeches. Mr. Trudeau directed their conception and planning; he took an active part in the drafting process, devoting much time to editorial review and meetings with his staff to go over texts, perhaps especially in this field. He also added much in the final presentation. There is no sense in which he was a talking head, merely mouthing the words of others without comprehension or commitment. And by the end of his period in office, the technical jargon and myriad details of most aspects of peace and security had become second nature to him; many experts who met with him would attest to this fact.

Most of Mr. Trudeau's speeches need little contextual introduction: they cannot be improved upon in this respect. However, it is probably useful to give the reader a brief presentation on each *grouping* of documents and to identify how they fit together. As well, the events which triggered and surrounded these comments may not always be apparent. For this reason, a select chronology of the Trudeau years from a Canadian foreign policy perspective is given at the end of the text.

To aid readers, I have inserted a number of explanatory footnotes where situations or terms referred to in Mr. Trudeau's remarks may prove unfamiliar or obscure.

It is probably too soon for a comprehensive and objective appraisal of the Trudeau legacy in the domestic and foreign policy fields. This book represents an interim step, a basis upon which others may build. Major assessments which *have* already been made by others are listed in the bibliography. My own reflections are set out in a final section which I wrote after several months of going over these materials.

In conclusion, I would like to thank Mel Hurtig, Elizabeth Munroe, and Jean Wilson of Hurtig Publishers, for their encouragement in this project; Mr. Trudeau for his immense kindness and good humour and editorial comments; Dr. Ian McClymont of the Prime Minister's Archives, Public Archives of Canada, for his practical help and advice; my wife, Gayle Jennings, for her unstinting support, acceptance of late nights at the library, and assistance with the selection of photographs; John Beaton of Canapress Photo Archives, for his patience while we searched the archives; and Cindy Zakoor of Accuword Pro, who typed the manuscript.

C. DAVID CRENNA

Chapter 1

Foundations of International Peace and Security

INTRODUCTION

anada has been called "the peaceable kingdom." It is the only nation on earth which has given up a nuclear arsenal and renounced the role of a nuclear power. It is the source of the "international peace-keeping force," and a leader in regional conflict resolution. Canada is simultaneously one of the least threatening nations on earth, the neighbour of a military colossus, the United States of America,* and the strategic terrain between the two superpowers, the U.S. and the Soviet Union.

In 1967, the Canadian sense of national identity reached a peak with a successful world's fair in Montreal and the celebration of a hundred years as a federation. In the wake of this euphoria, a new leader of the governing Liberal party, who automatically became Prime Minister, was elected at a party convention on April 6, 1968.

Pierre Elliott Trudeau was from both French and English cultures, had been educated in both languages, and had seen the world as student, traveller-adventurer, and legal scholar. He took power with both a determination, and the political necessity, to create some "distance" between his own Liberal ministry and that of his predecessor, Lester B. Pearson. The latter had never been given a clear majority of seats in the House of Commons. An integral part of the "new look" was a fundamental review of Canada's foreign policy, including defence, peace-keeping, arms control, and disarmament. The review was formally announced during the election campaign of May/June 1968.

The new policy direction responded to growing concern about superpower confrontation through their "intermediaries" in Vietnam, as well as scepticism about Canada's contribution to NATO in the light of resurgent European capacities. It also reflected as well the immediate past failures of middlepower "quiet diplomacy" faced with the Middle East and Southeast Asian conflicts. An overriding consideration was the domestic tension occasioned by the efforts

---

* Mr. Trudeau compared our relationship with the U.S. to sleeping next to an elephant.

of Quebec to build gradually a sovereign position through international links with France and other French-speaking countries.

The entire body of Mr. Trudeau's subsequent work on foreign policy would easily fill *two* books. This one concentrates on the subject of greatest continuing relevance and perhaps greatest intellectual innovation: international peace and security.

The Trudeau mind never placed the various topics of foreign affairs into isolated boxes. To him, efforts to promote peace and security had their foundations in relief from poverty and massive disparities in the wealth of nations. They were based on a clear appraisal of the dangers inherent in scientific endeavours as well as in politics. They took account of the robust forces of nationalism, even when they were cloaked in different ideological and cultural disguises.

This chapter presents statements from 1968 to 1975 which reveal the bedrock on which such later, innovative proposals as the strategy of "nuclear suffocation" and the "peace initiative" were based.

In his major foreign policy statement as Prime Minister, "Canada and the World" (pp. 4–8) Mr. Trudeau paid tribute to former Prime Minister Lester B. Pearson, but also made it clear that new plans were afoot that would link Canada's national interests more firmly with its foreign policy posture. Those "national interests," however, included the reduction of international tensions.

While they recognize his astuteness in diplomatic matters, there is an assumption among Mr. Trudeau's critics that he had little interest in or talent for defence policy. Yet he demonstrated again and again that he certainly understood defence forces as an element of diplomacy and as a bargaining counter in international relations. Perhaps what pained Mr. Trudeau's critics most was his sharp estimation of reasonable limits to the assignments Canadian forces could be given and what the Canadian public would support.

As is abundantly clear his speech in Calgary, Alberta (pp. 12–15), Mr. Trudeau wanted defence forces to be closely linked to foreign policy goals. Canada reduced its forces stationed in central Europe by half. Three aircraft squadrons were changed to a non-nuclear role and consolidated with the land forces in one location (Lahr, West Germany).

Mr. Trudeau's questions in Calgary foreshadowed his later argument that the Atlantic alliance must pursue *political* as well as military initiatives. The central thoughts which were fleshed out as the "peace initiative" of 1983–84 were first expressed in 1969.

More recently expressed concerns about the Strategic Defence Initiative also have deep roots. In March 1969, the Canadian government was caught somewhat off guard by a U.S. administration decision to deploy the Safeguard Anti-Ballistic Missile system (p. 16). There was controversy in both Washington and Ottawa about the adequacy of advance consultation. As it turned out, the Nixon Administration decided not to proceed with the new system and instead negotiated the ABM Treaty of 1972, which is still in force.

Mr. Trudeau expressed quite early the close link which exists between international aid to the Third World and the prospects for peace. In an address at the University of Alberta, he quoted Pope Paul VI: "The new name for peace is development..." (pp. 9–10).

A key contribution to improved world security in Mr. Trudeau's mind was the end of China's isolation. The Canadian overture to China was begun in the early 1960s, using the wheat trade, by Prime Minister John G. Diefenbaker and his engaging Minister of Agriculture, Alvin Hamilton.

Since then, the question of Chinese recognition had become entangled in the politics of the war in Vietnam. Another key stumbling block was the Chinese position that Canada could not simply recognize "two Chinas": a People's Republic of China and a Republic of China. The ensuing "Canadian formula" was later used by other countries: it "took note" of the mainland Chinese position that Taiwan was an "inalienable part of the territory of the People's Republic of China," but also recognized the People's Republic as "the sole legal government of China" (p. 17).

A key effort of the early Trudeau years was the improvement of Canada's ties with the Soviet Union which, in some respects, were less well-developed than those between the United States and its main rival. In 1971, Mr. Trudeau travelled to Moscow, the first Canadian Prime Minister to do so, and signed a protocol increasing consultations between the two neighbours (p.11).

Mr. Trudeau's desire to increase Canada's contacts with the major Communist powers was pragmatic, not ideological. He recognized more closely than most that human freedom was a fundamental basis for lasting peace, and he spoke of this eloquently in the "Mansion House" address of March 1975 (pp. 18–22).

Prompted by its long history of non-aggression, Canada has a reputation as an international "boy scout": it never does anything really wrong, is earnest in negotiations, but is somewhat naïve. Few incidents illustrated this better than the use by India of Canadian nuclear energy assistance to create its own atomic bomb.

The Indian atomic explosion of May 1974 blew away both a "special relationship" and a substantial amount of Canadian naïveté. Nuclear co-operation with that country was abruptly suspended; a new, stronger nuclear safeguard policy was developed and announced in December that year. Canada became much more active in promoting nuclear non-proliferation generally.* What Canada learned from bitter experience was summed up best in an address by Mr. Trudeau to the Canadian Nuclear Association (pp. 24–25).

These ideas: about a realistic middlepower role, a non-nuclear defence, a strong link between disarmament and development, improved relations with adversaries, a link between freedom and peace, and a desire to curb nuclear proliferation, constituted the essential planks on which later, more subtle and ambitious ideas rested. They may not have been unique to Mr. Trudeau, but they were nevertheless a refuge and an island of sanity in troubled times.

---

*Mr. Trudeau personally undertook a trip to Western Europe to urge government leaders there to sign the Nuclear Non-Proliferation Treaty. All the countries he visited subsequently subscribed to it.

STATEMENT BY THE PRIME MINISTER ON "CANADA AND THE WORLD"

OTTAWA, ONTARIO MAY 29, 1968

There is no reason for running down Canada's post-war record in international affairs. In many respects, it was a brilliant record, for which we owe much to the inspiring leadership of the Right Honourable Lester Pearson, both as External Affairs Minister and as Prime Minister.*

Reassessment has become necessary not because of the inadequacies of the past but because of the changing nature of Canada and of the world around us.

All of us need to ponder well what our national capacity is — what our potential may be — for participating effectively in international affairs. We shall do more good by doing well what we know to be within our resources to do, than by pretending either to ourselves or to others that we can do things clearly beyond our national capability.

Canada's position in the world is now very different from that of the post-war years. Then, we were probably the largest of the small powers. Our currency was one of the strongest. We were the fourth or fifth trading nation and our economy was much stronger than the European economies. Ours were among the very strongest navy and air forces. But now Europe has regained its strength. The Third World has emerged.

It is for us to decide whether and how we can make the best use abroad of the special skills, experience, and opportunities which our political, economic, and cultural evolution have produced in this rich and varied country.

Realism — that should be the operative word in our definition of international aim; realism is how we read the world barometer; realism is how we see ourselves thriving in the climate it forecasts. For we must begin with a concrete appraisal of the prevailing atmosphere — conscious always that rapid change is likely to be its chief characteristic.

What are some of the salient features we face?

The peace which we value most rests mainly on a balance of nuclear terror. Fortunately, the two superpowers have kept the terror firmly within their grasp and have been showing increasing responsibility about unleashing it. The threat of a major military clash has measurably receded, but not the need to ensure that the intricate power balance is maintained by a wide variety of means.

International tension is sustained in various regions and in varying degrees because of localized hostilities, latent disputes, racial discrimination, economic and social distress. Whatever comfort we can take from the most recent [peace feelers] in Vietnam, we dare not disregard the dangers inherent in the Middle East impasse, the race conflicts in the southern half of Africa, the heavy pressure of urgent needs in the developing world. In Europe, there remains the lingering threat of an unresolved German problem, which must be resolved if that continent is to capitalize on its growing desire to draw together and not turn once again down the dangerous road to aggressive nationalism.

---

*Mr. Pearson was Secretary of State for External Affairs between 1948 and 1957 and Prime Minister from 1963 to 1968.

It is no longer realistic to think in terms of a single model of organization and development in Eastern Europe or of a monolithic Communist unity such as Stalin could impose. There has been a perceptible détente in East-West relations. There has been a growing recognition in Eastern European countries of the need, through economic reforms, to adapt their economies to national needs, rather than adhere in a doctrinaire way to an economic model inspired largely by nineteenth-century conceptions.... [T]here are some fundamental and far-reaching differences between us and the Communist countries[;] it is no longer true to say that the Communist world is monolithically and implacably hostile to us.

Economic and social development continues to pose a major international problem, and it will increasingly engage the initiative, energy, and resources of the world community far into the future. The essential needs of the developing countries require a vigorous, comprehensive, and co-ordinated response from all the organizations, agencies, and individual nations seeking to alleviate the areas of want in the world. The realities of this North-South relation are such that humanity as a whole cannot rest easy until a steady and solid progress toward a better balance between have and have-not nations has been assured.

The international institutions and methods which have been adopted for dealing with the demands of the contemporary world situation have to be brought into closer alignment with actual development, and especially with the revolutionary desires of rising generations in all parts of the world. If man is to become the master rather than the victim of his restless genius for material progress, he must radically reduce the distance between his ever-advancing attainment in science and technology and the rather sluggish evolution of international instruments for maintaining political and economic order.

All round the earth, nations suffer the nervous exhaustion of living in an atmosphere of armed threat. It is risky enough that two superpowers, armed even now for "overkill," continue their competition for the most advanced weaponry. It does not help that secondary powers have embarked on nuclear-arms programmes.... [E]ven if it becomes possible to contain the nuclear competition, the world will still have to face what almost amounts to an unrestrained, and perhaps uncontrollable, traffic in conventional arms of all kinds, which, far from adding to security, tends to induce insecurity and increase tension.

In most of these international contexts, China continues to be both a colossus and a conundrum. Potentially, the People's Republic of China poses a major threat to peace, largely because calculations about Chinese ambitions, intentions, capacity to catch up, and even about actual developments within China have to be based on incomplete information — which opens an area of unpredictability. Mainland China's exclusion from the world community stems partly from policies of non-recognition and of seeking to contain Chinese Communism through military means, and partly from Peking's own policies and problems. Yet most of the major world issues to which I have referred will not be resolved completely, or in any lasting way, unless and until an accommodation has been reached with the Chinese nation.

Those are the broad lines of the international environment in which Canada finds itself today. What are we proposing to do about it? We are going to begin with a thorough and comprehensive review of our foreign policy which embraces defence, economic, and aid policies. Policy review is part of the normal process of any government, but we wish to take a fresh look at the fundamentals of Canadian foreign policy to see whether there are ways in which we can serve more effectively Canada's current interests, objectives, and priorities.

Our approach will be pragmatic and realistic — above all, to see that our policies in the future accord with our national needs and resources, with our ability to discharge Canada's legitimate responsibilities in world affairs.

Our progressive involvement in international development and relations during two decades or more has given this country a position of prominence and distinction. The policy area to be reviewed is broad and complex....

We as a Government must discharge our duty to the people of Canada in meeting the needs of national security. In the narrowest sense, this could mean the strengthening of North American defence arrangements in a manner calculated to safeguard our national sovereignty and at the same time to make the best use of resources allocated to national defence. But the defence strategies of our time are neither static nor restricted in scope. NATO and NORAD, though not linked organizationally, are complementary in their strategic importance and implication. They are an integral part of the delicate balance of power on which the peace of the world has rested during a long and difficult period. We shall take a hard look, in consultation with our allies, at our military role in NATO and determine whether our present military commitment is still appropriate to the present situation in Europe. We shall look at our role in NORAD in the light of the technological advances of modern weaponry and of our fundamental opposition to the proliferation of nuclear weapons.

Canada continues to have a very large stake in Europe, perhaps not so much in the military sense of two decades ago but in political, commercial, and cultural terms. We have been fascinated and greatly encouraged by the marked improvements in the political and economic situation in Europe as a whole, in both the Eastern and Western sectors. It seems almost axiomatic that, far from relaxing them, Canada should seek to strengthen its ties with the European nations, whose many and varied cultures contribute so much of our own. We should seek to join with them in new forms of partnership and co-operation in order to strengthen international security, to promote economic stability on both sides of the Atlantic and in other regions of the world, to balance our own relations in the Western Hemisphere.

We have a major aim of maintaining mutual confidence and respect in our relations with the United States. We have to sort out the dilemmas which that complex relation poses for us so as to widen the area of mutual benefit without diminishing our Canadian identity and sovereign independence.

We have to take greater account of the ties which bind us to other nations in this Hemisphere — in the Caribbean, Latin America — and of their economic needs. We have to explore new avenues of increasing our political and economic relations with Latin America, where more than 400 million people will live by the turn of the century and where we have substantial interests.

We accept as a heavy responsibility of higher priority Canada's participation in programmes for the economic and social development of nations in the developing areas. We shall be exploring all means of increasing the impact of our aid programmes by concentrating on places and projects in which our bilingualism, our own expertise and experience, our resources and facilities make possible an effective and distinctively Canadian contribution. We see Africa as an area of growing activity, but not to the exclusion of other regions in which Canada's aid effort is well established. We intend, moreover, to combine these efforts with initiatives, policies, and leadership relating to trade which will enable the developing nations to attain lasting improvement in their economies.

We shall be guided by considerations such as the foregoing in sustaining our support for international organizations — and especially the United Nations family. We believe that Canada's contribution to the co-operative efforts of those organizations may benefit from some shift of emphasis, but there will be no slackening of our broad policy of support. In making our reappraisal, we shall be looking for realistic means for making multilateral organizations as effective as possible and, correspondingly, Canada's participation in their endeavours.

We shall be looking at our policy in relation to China in the context of a new interest in Pacific affairs generally. Because of past preoccupations with Atlantic and European affairs, we have tended to overlook the reality that Canada is a Pacific country, too. Canada has long advocated a positive approach to mainland China and its inclusion in the world community. We have an economic interest in trade with China — no doubt shared by others — and a political interest in preventing tension between China and its neighbours, but especially between China and the United States. Our aim will be to recognize the People's Republic of China Government as soon as possible and to enable that Government to occupy the seat of China in the United Nations, taking into account that there is a separate government in Taiwan.

. . . [I]n reviewing the international situation and our external policies, we are likely to find that many of the problems are the same ones which Canada has faced for many years — global and regional tensions, underdevelopment, economic disruptions. Our broad objectives may be similar, too — the maintenance of peace and security, the expansion and improvement of aid programmes, the search for general economic stability. But what we shall be looking for — systematically, realistically, pragmatically — will be new approaches, new methods, new opportunities. In that search we shall be seeking the views of Canadians, and particularly of those with expert knowledge in the universities and elsewhere.

We shall hope, too, to find new attitudes, for ourselves and in others, which will give us the latitude to make progress in the pursuit of those objectives. There is much evidence of a desire for this kind of change in most countries of the world. Our need is not so much to go crusading abroad as to mobilize at home our aspirations, energies, and resources behind external policies which will permit Canada to play a credible and creditable part in this changing world.

To do this we need not proclaim our independence. We need not preach to others or castigate them. What we need do is to be sure that we are being as effective as we can be in carrying out our own commitments and responsibilities, which will be commensurate with our growing status and strength, with our special character.

What is our paramount interest in pursuing this kind of foreign policy? Well, the foreign policies of nations are grounded in history and geography and culture. There are very obvious major interests for most nations today — peace, prosperity, and progress of all kinds. There is always a substantial element of self-interest. In this general sense, Canada is no exception.

But at the present time . . . our paramount interest is to ensure the political survival of Canada as a federal and bilingual sovereign state. This means strengthening Canadian unity as a basically North American country. It means reflecting in our foreign relations the cultural diversity and the bilingualism of

Canada as faithfully as possible. Parallel to our close ties with the Commonwealth, we should strive to develop a close relation with the [French-speaking] countries....

[W]e have taken some immediate steps which will give the Canadian people an indication of the direction the Government will follow....

STATEMENT BY THE PRIME MINISTER, PIERRE ELLIOTT TRUDEAU, TO A CONVOCATION CEREMONY, DIAMOND JUBILEE OF THE UNIVERSITY OF ALBERTA

EDMONTON, MAY 13, 1968

Never before in history has the disparity between the rich and the poor, the comfortable and the starving, been so extreme; never before have mass communications so vividly informed the sufferers of the extent of their misery; never before have the privileged societies possessed weapons so powerful that their employment in the defence of privilege would destroy the haves and the have-nots indiscriminately. We are faced with an overwhelming challenge. In meeting it, the world must be our constituency.

I can find no better words to express this view than those employed in General Principle Four of the Final Act of the 1964 United Nations Conference on Trade and Development: "Economic development and social progress should be the common concern of the whole international community and should, by increasing economic prosperity and well-being, help strengthen peaceful relations and co-operation among nations."

Pope Paul VI in his fifth encyclical was even more concise: "the new name for peace is development...."

These references to assistance and to co-operation relate not only to economic assistance. They relate to assistance in any form that will create the political, economic, and human climate most conducive to the nurturing of human dignity. International activities of this breadth are a far cry from the earlier and more primitive concepts of direct financial assistance. In their impact and in their value, they are also a long way from charity philanthropy. If the Canadian goal is to assist other states in this way, then we are involved with humanity. And we are involved for our mutual benefit.

I emphasize this because when one benefits from an activity one is less likely to object to its cost. How do we benefit? In several aspects:

(a) A world community of nations freely co-operating should result in a lessening of international tension. This would lead to a world less suscepti-ble to war. Canada and Canadians would become more secure, and in this troubled world, that would be a benefit beyond measure.

(b) A multiplicity of nations possessing expanding economies would mean that standards of living would rise and world markets would multiply. Canadian products would find more purchasers, and for a trading nation such as Canada, that would be a benefit of great value.

(c) In times of peace, men have turned their attention toward the development of their cultures, and the enrichment of life. Canadians live more meaning-fully by enjoying the works of artists and scholars of whatever national source, and that is a benefit of unquestioned value.

These interests and these benefits submit to no national boundaries. The social, economic, and political betterment of any man anywhere is ultimately reflected in this country. If at the same time our consciences — our humanitarian instincts — are served... then so much the better. Unquestionably the concept of international assistance is appealing because it is one of the most uplifting endeavours in which man has ever engaged. But we must never forget that in this process, Canadians are beneficiaries as well as benefactors....

The long-range benefits cannot be overemphasized.... [I]nternational co-operation, particularly in the field of economic assistance, in order to remain effective must take on a new form. From the present pattern of commodity and food assistance, of gifts of manufactured goods and loans of money, we must, in response to the economic needs of the developing countries, turn more and more to preferential trade arrangements. The two United Nations Conferences on Trade and Development have made clear that economic aid, in order to be effective, must increasingly take the form of trade.

[T]hese preferential trade arrangements have no glamour attached to them. They cannot be illustrated by stirring photographs of rugged Canadian engineers posing before massive dams in remote places. This kind of aid doesn't offer a ready market to Canadian manufacturers, nor does it reduce our base metal or other commodity surpluses.* In short, this kind of aid is competition, and bears little evidence of the sweet philanthropy which we have sometimes employed in the past to coat the cost of our aid "pill." Unless Canadians are aware of the vital goal our aid is seeking to achieve, they may not be sympathetic to a change of this sort. It is my opinion [that] Canadians will understand and will accept the challenge. Economic aid, unless effective, will be useless. In order to be effective it will, in all likelihood, be costly. Yet we and the other developed nations have no alternative. The world cannot continue to accommodate mutually exclusive blocs of rich nations and poor nations.

We must recognize that, in the long run, the overwhelming threat to Canada will not come from foreign investments, or foreign ideologies, or even — with good fortune — foreign nuclear weapons. It will come instead from the two-thirds of the peoples of the world who are steadily falling farther and farther behind in their search for a decent standard of living. This is the meaning of the revolution of rising expectations. I repeat, this problem is not new. But its very size, involving some two-and-a-half billion people, makes it qualitatively different from what it has been in the past....

---

*This is a reference to the fact that a portion of Canadian aid is often tied to purchases of Canadian equipment and supplies.

EXCERPTS FROM A STATEMENT BY THE PRIME MINISTER IN THE HOUSE OF COMMONS ON POLICY TOWARD THE SOVIET UNION

MAY 28, 1971

The relations between Canada and the Soviet Union in the postwar years have not all been of a wholesome or a desirable nature. I harbour no naïve belief that, as a result of this [new] protocol, [signed between Canada and the U.S.S.R.] our two countries will find themselves suddenly in a relation that will reflect nothing but sweetness and tender feelings.... [T]here remain many fundamental differences between us: differences relating to deep-seated concerns springing from historic, geographic, ideological, economic, social, and military factors.*

But surely the only way to resolve these differences and eliminate these concerns is by increased contact and effort at understanding. That is what the protocol proposes. That is what, in a different way, is achieved by prime ministerial visits. Through them an opportunity is created by the pens of journalists and the cameras of photographers for the people of both Canada and the Soviet Union to learn much more about one another — their respective histories, their sufferings, their aspirations....

Only time will tell whether the warm welcome which was accorded me in the U.S.S.R. reflects the commencement of an era in Canadian-Soviet relations as advantageous as we all hope will be the case. I prefer to be optimistic and I am urging all government departments to exploit these new openings. I urge Canadian businessmen to accept the new challenge. For our part as Canadians, I assured the Soviet leaders that there was no impediment in our desire for better and more mutually beneficial relations.

---

*Canada only recognized the Soviet Union in 1942. The famous "Gouzenko" affair of 1949 — a widespread KGB spy network was revealed by a cipher clerk in the Soviet Embassy who defected — soured relations for many years.

STATEMENT BY THE PRIME MINISTER, PIERRE ELLIOTT TRUDEAU, TO THE ALBERTA LIBERAL ASSOCIATION

CALGARY, APRIL 12, 1969*

...Our defence budget... is one-sixth of the total budget. That's a lot of money — $1,800 million for defence. And it's a lot of money especially when you realize that it's accompanied by a great deal of uncertainty on the part of Canadians.

There has been a tendency in the past few years... to say to the Federal Government, "Spend less on defence, you'll have more for this other worthwhile project" — whether it be education or health or housing or urban growth.... There has been a tendency [to imply] ... that the money we spent on defence [was] not well spent.

Now this may be so, and if it is so, it is important that we correct it. It is important that we realize that the sixth of our national budget which is spent on defence is not... accepted as justifiable by a significant proportion of the Canadian people — and even the military themselves.

Well, what should we do about it? Are we spending too much money or are we spending too little? This is the kind of question we have been asking ourselves in Ottawa....

What we want to do with this $1,800 million is to defend Canadian sovereignty and to contribute to world peace. Why else would Canadians want to spend money on defence? We don't want to go to war with anybody. [The aim] of our foreign policy [is] to serve our national interests.... [W]hen I say national interests, I am not thinking in any egotistical sense of just what's happening to Canadians. It's in our national interest to reduce the tensions in the world, tensions which spring from the two-thirds of the world's population who go to bed hungry every night... and the tensions which spring from this great ideological struggle between East and West.

[T]he aim of our foreign policy... is [also] to express our national identity abroad so that the other countries know us. So they know what we stand for, know what our interests and our values are, in the economic sphere, in the cultural sphere, in the social sphere, in the ideological sphere. This is what our foreign policy is all about....

[T]he strategic factors making for peace or threatening war have changed immensely in a generation.... [T]he existence of [Soviet ballistic missiles] which are pre-targeted on all the major European and North American cities and which can spell immediate destruction if they are ever unleashed is a new factor.... [T]here is a very delicate balance, a balance of deterrent forces, between the two poles of military strength on this planet of today, and this is a new factor....

Before the Second World War, as it is said, we practically had no [distinct] foreign policy; we were too small a country in terms of population and in wealth, and our foreign policy wasn't very different from that of the United

---

* Mr. Trudeau has edited this speech slightly.

States or of the United Kingdom, providing they had the same foreign policy.... [W]hen their interests diverged... well, we tacked onto one or onto the other....

After the Second World War, we were faced with a Europe which was divided into two [hostile] power blocks... a Europe which had been impoverished and destroyed by war.... [W]e realized that the tensions in Europe could be the most destructive ones for a lasting peace.... [A]long with other countries, realizing the principal threat to peace was Soviet aggression, we helped set up NATO as an answer to that possibility of aggression....

Twenty years later, today, Europe has been rebuilt. The gross national product of the NATO countries in Europe is over $500 billion. The population, 300 million people. Canada's contribution to this Europe, important though it has been and important though it remains, is marginal — 20 million people against 300 million. Our defence policy, which flowed from this foreign policy of NATO, now [is] more to impress our friends than frighten our enemies. Our contribution... is marginal now in terms of strict military strength — one mechanized division against perhaps 80 or 55, depending on how you count them.... It is important; I am not trying to belittle it.

But we have to remain free to decide our own foreign policy. And when we are told that we shouldn't be taking a free ride to peace in the world, when we are told that if we withdraw from NATO even in any degree this will lead other countries to withdraw from NATO, I don't admit this. I don't admit that Europeans or even Americans won't follow their own wisdom, that they don't have their own foreign policy. And I don't admit that our friends and allies will be guided in their decisions and determined in their actions by what Canadians do.... [W]e are entitled, we have a right, to ask questions about our participation in NATO.

In 1949, when we set up NATO, I think it was true that we could not wait for political settlements in order to meet the security issue, because the security issue was the number one issue. But 20 years later, I should be inclined to say that we can't wait until all the problems of security have been settled before we tackle the political issue of peace in the world. And it so happened that NATO after 20 years, in our opinion, had developed too much into a military alliance... not enough into a political alliance, not enough into an alliance which [was] interested not only in keeping the balance of deterrence... in Europe, but into an alliance which [was] interested in arms control and de-escalation.

...I am afraid, in the situation which we had reached, NATO had in reality determined all of our defence policy.... And our defence policy had determined all of our foreign policy.... [T]his is a false perspective for any country. It is a false perspective to have a military alliance determine your foreign policy. It should be your foreign policy which determines your military policy.

So all we have done... was to stand the pyramid on its base. It was standing on its head. We have decided to review our foreign policy and to have a defence policy flow from that.... In our statement last week, we said that the first priority for Canadians was not NATO, important though it be... to remain aligned in NATO with those countries who believe in deterring the Soviet aggression in Europe.... Our first priority is the protection of Canadian sovereignty, in all its dimensions.

I don't accept the criticism of those who say this is a return to isolationism, or this is a return to the "fortress America" concept. This is not our purpose....

What we are doing in our foreign policy, and...in our defence policy, we shall do after discussing with our allies, and we shall explain to them that our contribution is in order to promote the values which they are promoting in NATO — values of freedom and of liberty....

But it is false to talk of isolationism when you think of Canada, which is territorially one of the largest countries in the world...and which has a very small population in terms of the middle and great powers. It is absurd to say that this is isolationism because we are not on all the fronts of the world, political and military, fighting with other people. You can't talk of isolationism of Canadians because, with the small manpower we have, with the economic means we have, we say we want to use the first part of it in terms of our own sovereignty, the second part of it in terms of the defence of our territory and of the continent, and the third part of it in defence of other alliances such as NATO, such as peace-keeping operations which we will embark upon and have embarked upon through the United Nations. We need our armed forces in order to perform these roles, but in degrees determined by our foreign policy. We don't want a military alliance or a defence policy to pre-empt all our choices....

We have a right to ask questions of our allies. If they want to keep us on these terms we shall be very happy because [we want to keep] our friends in NATO. We want to continue "dialoguing" with them in the political sense. We want to keep these channels of communication open.... It's right now, I believe, that we ask questions of ourselves about NATO and we ask questions of our allies about NATO.

Is an armoured brigade the right kind of contribution Canadians should make to Europe, could make to NATO? Is an armoured brigade, which can only be used in the plains of northern Germany, the right kind of contribution for Canadians to make? Is our squadron of CF-104s, which can be armed with conventional bombs or with nuclear bombs, the right kind of contribution? And what is the scenario for using nuclear arms in Europe, in our bombers, in our CF-104s? Do we want to participate in this way in an alliance without knowing in which way these so-called [nuclear] tactical weapons will be used? Are the Soviets...not entitled to ask themselves: "Are [the CF-104 fighters] going to be first strike or second strike? They are soft targets, they are on the ground, we know where the airfields are. Isn't it likely that they might be used to attack us first?" These are the questions that our enemies, the Soviets, are asking themselves, and these are the questions we are asking of our allies.

Our contribution in the naval area to anti-submarine warfare — is this the right contribution? Should we be having the kind of naval force which is prepared to destroy the Soviet nuclear-armed submarines, which are a deterrent for them as the *Polaris* is a deterrent for the United States? The United States has *Polaris* submarines in the ocean and will use them if it is attacked first. If the American cities are destroyed, the Americans know that they have their submarines as a second-strike capacity.... This is part of the balance of terror. This permits the Americans to say to the Soviets: "If you start first, we can still destroy you with our submarines." The [Soviet and American] submarines... by nature, I suppose, [have] this capacity — they are second strike, they are deterrent. Is our policy right to be armed essentially against them? [Is it not destabilizing to threaten to destroy the deterrent?]

These are the questions we want to ask of our allies, and we want to decide what our contribution in NATO will be. I am not promising any revolutionary changes. There may be some and they may not be very great. But . . . whatever our contribution will be in a military sense will flow from our foreign policy. . . .

REMARKS FOLLOWING QUESTION PERIOD ON THE U.S. ANTI-BALLISTIC MISSILE SYSTEM

OTTAWA, MARCH 17, 1969

Q. What is your personal reaction [to the U.S. announcement of a plan to deploy the Safeguard Anti-Ballistic Missile System]?

A. Well...my personal reaction is that we don't want anything which would escalate the danger of war and escalate the arms race. The question is: how do you assess this latest step by the Americans? Is it an escalation, or is it a keeping-up with what the Russians have done outside of Moscow....

Q. What was the point you were making, Sir, about the interests of humanity being ahead of the interests of a few Canadian cities?

A. Well, I was being asked by the Opposition if we had negotiated with the Americans on the location of these ABM system missiles and I indicated that that wasn't our first concern, that if this defence system was ever brought into use, this would indicate the failure of peace-keeping and this might indicate the end of the world. My first concern was not in trying to get a little more protection for Canadian soil, a few miles further north or a few miles further south, it was the question which was being asked to me by the Opposition, did we negotiate on the location of these ABMs. I was saying that before trying to negotiate on the location of the ABMs, it was more important to make up our minds if we were going to condemn or approve the system altogether. It's secondary only that we would think of Canadian cities. We were first concerned with the peace of the world....

NEW ZEALAND INSTITUTE OF INTERNATIONAL AFFAIRS PANEL DISCUSSION

VICTORIA UNIVERSITY OF WELLINGTON, MAY 13, 1970

Q. We have heard over recent months that Canada has initiated a series of afternoon teas between yourselves and the People's Republic of China.... You obviously need China, but what grounds have you for thinking the Chinese need you?

A. Well...we don't need China in any strictly material sense.... China has been one of our great trading partners before there was any question of diplomatic exchange between the Peking Government and ourselves. We were selling very substantial quantities of wheat and...other goods to China.... [I]f it were strictly from the trade point of view it might have been better to leave well enough alone because...if the negotiations went very badly, we might have stirred up a question which we would regret. So in that sense we don't need China. Perhaps China needs us, at least it did in the years of drought and bad crops.... [O]ne of the facts of life was that the PROC was the Government of something like a quarter of all mankind and...we felt we could not continue playing the game of pretending they didn't exist in the society of nations....

So that is why we are doing it — because of its potential, because of its advance in many fields, [because it] is a very important partner in the human dialogue. We believe that politics within a country and within the world can only be based on understanding, on communication. We don't think it's possible to get everyone to agree to the same ideology and to the same postulates, but we do think it is necessary for each participant to understand the point of view of the other....

We're saying [through recognition] there is a China. The question is what is the legitimate government of China? Is it the one that sits in Peking, is it the one that sits in Taipei?... [W]e're telling the Peking Government that we're not recognizing its territorial claim [to Taiwan] in the same sense that when we recognized Bonn, we were not determining the issue whether Bonn has a right to claim sovereignty over all of East Germany....

NOTES FOR REMARKS BY THE
PRIME MINISTER AT THE MANSION HOUSE

LONDON, MARCH 13, 1975

In no other country in the world has the concept of "freedom" been so debated, its meaning so extended, its practice so protected [as in Great Britain].

To be a free man anywhere is a condition of great moment, but to be a free man in England — to breathe Lord Mansfield's pure air — is more; it is an exhilarating experience.

Through the centuries, man's quest for freedom has varied in its focus as tyranny has assumed new forms and threatened it from new quarters. On one occasion the tyrant has been the Crown, on another the Church; at one moment the threat proceeded from a domestic source, at the next it came from without the realm.

Throughout this tireless and changing pursuit of freedom, the attainments of the British people have become the standards against which men and women world-wide have measured their own accomplishments. The milestones of Magna Carta and habeas corpus, the Petition of Right and the Bill of Rights, have become models for societies everywhere; they turned the tide of battle in favour of the classical freedoms — of speech, of conscience, of association, of assembly. Yet the result has not been permanent social tranquility, in England or elsewhere. Nor should we be surprised. I doubt that any of those great observers of the English scene — Bracton or Locke or Burke or Bagehot — ever believed that political freedom would not, and should not, be employed to seek the betterment of other aspects of the human condition. And such has been the case. Having established firmly the principle of the positive freedoms — the freedoms "of" — we now find ourselves involved in a struggle to establish with equal sanctity the negative freedoms — the freedoms "from": from want, from hunger, from disease, from nuclear holocaust, from environmental degradation.

And we find that this struggle is more complex, more awkward, and more wide-ranging than we had thought possible. There is no single tyrant here; no evil King, no zealot of the Church against whom we can focus our energies and direct our strategies. Equally, there is no immediate and identifiable challenge to our well-being that can be laid low with a single outburst of passion and courage: no St. Crispin's Day, no Trafalgar, no Star Chamber advocacy. What involves us today is a struggle of far greater proportions yet with far fewer handles for men and women to grasp. It is not the absence from the scene today of a Pitt or a Churchill that causes men and women to wonder in what direction humanity is pointed; it is the nature of the adversary. More than eloquence and more than leadership is required to come to grips with monetary imbalances, nutritional deficiencies, and environmental pollution. Not a Shakespeare or a Wordsworth or a Kipling could translate into stirring words the requirements for commodity price stabilization or nuclear non-proliferation. Yet these struggles are the essence of life on this planet today. They are not struggles that can be confined to a law court or a battlefield or a House of Commons; they require institutions and regimes of immense dimensions and novel attributes; they call — in the final analysis — for world-wide co-operation, for they demand that we struggle not against other human beings but with other human beings. They demand a common cause of humanity.

In this cause we all — Britons and Canadians — have a vital role to play. We must not assume, however, that that role is dictated by altruism any more than we should think of it as selfish. It is in our interest, as it is our obligation, to contribute our skills and our experience and our disciplines to the solution of the immense problems which face mankind today and which threaten freedom in new and unprecedented ways. These problems will require of us decisions no less courageous and no less momentous than those faced by the barons of the early 13th century as they drafted the Magna Carta. Yet those decisions, if wisely taken, will have an impact on the world no less startling and no less lasting than that of the Magna Carta. For now, as in 1215, the world is ready for those decisions.

Professor J.C. Holt has written of Magna Carta: "The barons did not talk of free men out of loftiness of purpose, or make concessions to knights and burgesses out of generosity. They did so because the political situation required it and because the structure of English society and government allowed them to do no other."

It is my submission that now, 760 years after the event at Runnymede, the changes that must be incorporated into the international system can be justified in similar language: "The political situation requires it; the structure of world society and institutions allows us to do no other."

We have at this moment in time an opportunity to recognize and arrest the inertia which threatens to plunge all too many societies into a vast labyrinth of confusion and despair. The first step in that process is acceptance of two facts: the inter-relationship of all countries, and the interconnection of all phenomena. The acceptance, in brief, of what each of the world's cultures has been proclaiming for centuries — that we are all brothers.

Only recently has evidence emerged establishing beyond doubt that this brotherhood exists in the realm of actuality as well as in the realm of theology. The evidence is a product of human accomplishment. Man's past successes in removing so many of the great barriers of distance and time and mystery have created a world far different than that known in previous centuries, or in previous decades. It is different because those old barriers hindered more than migration. They defined the natural limitations of conquering armies, of famine and plague, of catastrophes, both natural and man-made.

Today those barriers are gone. There are no bulwarks behind which we can retreat in order to stave off or avoid calamity from abroad. And if there are any who believe otherwise, they are fools. Nations which are told that they can exist and flourish independent of the world are being misinformed. Leaders and opinion-makers who claim the existence of simple solutions to sweeping issues have forfeited their claim to office, be it in Whitehall or Fleet Street or Russell Square. Citizens who accept uncritically such siren songs are not discharging their responsibility as free men and women in democratic societies.

We are one on this earth. Each has the power to injure all others. Each of us must assume the responsibility that that implies. And each must understand that the nature of that injury is not ephemeral and it is not transient. It can be real and it can be permanent. Co-operation is no longer simply advantageous; in order to survive it is an absolute necessity.

Yet ironically and fortunately, it is this very situation which is so promising, as was a different situation so promising to clear-eyed men in 1215. Fearful though I am of the havoc that will be the inevitable result of continued selfishness and indifference, I am far from despondent, for I believe in the human quality of man's instincts and in the essentially rational behaviour of which he is capable.

Those instincts have lifted him from a solitary hunting animal to an intensely social being, aware of the advantages that flow from co-operation and from the sharing of tasks, aware of the benefits that follow when new structures are set in place to facilitate that co-operation. The history of mankind has been shaped in large measure by men and women who have acted as architects of social organization. Their works remain on view in the simplest villages and in the largest metropolises.

Remaining as well for historians to assess are those accomplishments of international organization — and the equally grand failures — which have marked the past three decades. In many instances these institutions are still too new, still not sufficiently formed, to permit final judgement. Even while pursuing the understandable and altogether proper desire for evolution and modification, the instinct which lay behind the original plan demands praise . . . .

The extension . . . of co-operation among industrialized nations, and the creation of co-operative institutions are important functions and necessary ones. Yet however well-designed and sturdily built, these structures will crumble away and be regarded by historians of the future with the same air of detachment now visited upon archeological ruins if they are not extended still further and made global in their reach and in the distribution of their benefits. Happily, this very extension is now underway. There has been a step toward redemption of promises extended on several occasions that the European Community would not submit to the temptation and false luxury of looking only inward.

In recent days, an historic agreement has been concluded between the Community and a number of developing countries. This agreement is an admirable contribution to the resolution of the broad differences which currently exist in the attitudes of many of the developing and industrialized countries toward the international economic structure.

The demands of the developing countries have been carefully formulated and powerfully articulated. They reflect a sense of frustration and anger. Those countries seek no piecemeal adjustments, but a comprehensive restructuring of all the components — fiscal, monetary, trade, transport, and investment. The response of the industrialized countries can be no less well-prepared and no less comprehensive in scope. But we should be very wrong, and do ourselves and our children a great disservice, if we regarded this process as an adversary one. We would be foolish as well, for solutions are not beyond our reach.

The human community is a complex organism linked again and again within itself and as well with the biosphere upon which it is totally dependent for life. This interdependency demands of us two functions: first, the maintenance of an equilibrium among all our activities, whatever their nature; second, an equitable distribution, world-wide, of resources and opportunities.

The proper discharge of those functions calls for more than tinkering with the present system. The processes required must be global in scope and universal in application. In their magnitude, if not in their concept, they must be new. Of their need, none can doubt.

We know in our hearts what has to be done if we have not yet found in our minds the way it can be done.

Let us begin to search, and let us do so with boldness and with excitement, not with hesitancy and uncertainty. The past quarter century of increased political independence, increased industrial development, increased commercial trade, and increased affluence was not the product of timid men. Nor will be the accomplishments of the forthcoming period of total interdependence.

The key, as in all accomplishments of worth, lies within the scope of individual men and women. It is found in their attitudes toward others. The role of leadership today is to encourage the embrace of a global ethic. An ethic that abhors the present imbalance in the basic human condition — an imbalance in access to health care, to a nutritious diet, to shelter, to education. An ethic that extends to all men, to all space, and through all time. An ethic that is based on confidence in one's fellow man. Confidence that with imagination and discipline the operation of the present world economic structure can be revised to reflect more accurately the needs of today and tomorrow. Confidence that those factors which have the effect of discriminating against the developing countries can be removed from the world's trading and monetary systems. Confidence that we can create a trading order which is truly universal and not confined to or favouring groups defined along geographic or linguistic or ideological or religious or any other lines. Confidence that access to liquidity for trade and for development will not be restricted by factors other than those accepted by all as necessary in order to contribute to the health of the entire world system.

In the calculation of this new balance, we must aim for nothing less than an acceptable distribution of the world's wealth. In doing so, the inequities resulting from the accidental location of valuable geological formations should no more be overlooked than should the present unequal acquisition of technological and managerial skills. Nor should we be reluctant in encouraging those willing to help themselves. We must encourage and offer incentives to peoples who — given the opportunity — are willing to exercise self-discipline, to demonstrate tolerance, to work industriously.

The attainment of a goal of wealth distribution does not require the replacement of the present international monetary system, nor does it require a wholesale abandonment of the trading mechanisms employed with such success in the past, and which have brought unprecedented levels of prosperity to increasing numbers of persons in all countries in the world. It does require, however, imagination and ingenuity and hard work....

These needs are all challenges...but they should not be regarded as the gloomy prospect of avoiding doomsday. Properly met, they can be joyous opportunities permitting the introduction into the world of a dynamic equilibrium between man and nature, between man and man. The challenge is a challenge of sharing: of good, of technology, of resources, of scientific knowledge. None need do without if all will become good stewards of what we have. And to ensure that, we must concentrate not so much on what we possess but on what we are and what we are capable of becoming.

What I dare to believe is that men and women everywhere will come to understand that no individual, no government, no nation is capable of living in isolation, or of pursuing policies inconsistent with the interests — both present and future — of others. That self-respect is not self-perpetuating but depends for its existence on access to social justice. That each of us must do all in our power to extend justice. That each of us must do all in our power to extend to all persons an equal measure of human dignity — to ensure through our efforts that hope and faith in the future are not reserved for a minority of the world's population, but are available to all.

This responsibility rests on each one of us. It is not transferable. Its discharge is not conditional upon the acts or the omissions of others. It demands that we care; that we share; that we be honest.

In this global village we are all accountable.

None of us can escape the burden of our responsibility. None of us can escape the tragedy of any failure. Nor, happily, will anyone escape the benefit, the joy, the satisfaction — the freedom — which will accompany the discharge of that responsibility.

EXCERPTS FROM REMARKS BY THE PRIME MINISTER TO THE ANNUAL MEETING OF THE CANADIAN NUCLEAR ASSOCIATION

OTTAWA, JUNE 17, 1975*

It would be much easier if we lived in a world where science had not yet removed so many of the great mysteries which once defined and limited the power of men. It would be easier if — ; there would be less need if — . But "ifs" are not available to us. History, it has been said, is not written in the subjunctive.

Which is to say that we must live with reality. It is reality that tells us that seldom elsewhere is there such a confluence of events and interests and issues as in the nuclear field. Here, we find ourselves in possession at the same moment of technology of the most revolutionary and serviceable kind, technology which has proved to all the world Canada's competence and leadership. Here, too, we are engaged in a mineral industry of immense economic benefit, yet of staggering production costs and problems. And here we face dangers of the most awesome sort, exceeding in risk and potential destruction any knowledge ever possessed by human beings.

With stakes so valuable and knowledge so changing, with consequences so sweeping and issues so baffling in their moral and ethical application, there should be little wonder that answers are not always available, or not always acceptable when they are available.

Nuclear activity is one of the many in which man is now engaged which, if not made susceptible to reason and discipline, could become ultra-hazardous, even cataclysmic. All of our joint wisdom and all of our dedication will be required in order to ensure that mankind enjoys the benefits of this activity without suffering from its perils. Canadian government nuclear policies have attempted to steer this course. . . . [W]e are traversing uncharted terrain where a wrong turn could engulf us in holocaust. We have no alternative but caution because our tolerance for error and our ability to reverse miscalculation are minimal.

Familiarity with nuclear processes and confidence in their peaceful benefits must never blind us to the destructive capability of a nuclear explosive device or the politically destabilizing effect that can be caused in certain circumstances by the mere existence of such a device. . . . [N]o matter how sincere is our commitment to equality throughout the world, no matter how successful is our progress toward it, our achievements will be Pyrrhic should nations be unable to avoid the inhumanity of nuclear weapons usages or threats.

It is an enigma that surely no sane observer could untangle — this nuclear threat to the very continuance of the human race that has become so common-place as to be boring, that is often regarded in some perverse fashion as a symbol of national accomplishment and well-being or as a manifestation of sovereignty.

No nation should be envious of another because it possesses the ability to kill hundreds of thousands of human beings in a single explosion. No nation should

---

*Parts of this speech originally delivered in French; here translated into English.

treasure its power to trigger a nuclear war. And no nation should misinterpret Canada's opposition to proliferation as envy of foreign accomplishments.

Canada is not envious of any country that is able to achieve new scientific plateaux for the benefit of its peoples nor, to my knowledge, is any other industrialized state. If a newly independent nation is able to leap in a single generation from the stage of steam to the age of the atom, Canada applauds. If that leap was accomplished through Canadian assistance, we are proud. But the vault must be genuine, and the new plateau must be firm. Nuclear projects have proved their benefit to man in dozens of ways — ways well known to most of you — but no one has yet demonstrated convincingly that there are practical, economic, peaceful benefits of nuclear explosions. Not Americans, not Russians, not Indians. If at some time in the future such benefits be demonstrated, then they should be made available on an internationally accepted basis, under appropriate safeguards, and through a UN agency, to all countries declared by international experts as able to benefit. Canada is opposed to any peaceful nuclear explosions not conducted in accordance with the provisions of the N.P.T.* In doing so we are not imputing motives; we are attempting to avoid the subjunctive.

These are the reasons why Canada signed the Non-Proliferation Treaty, why I seize every opportunity to garner the support of world leaders for a tightening and an extension of safeguards and controls. These are the reasons why we will continue to do so.

Each one of us shares a common desire: to turn over to our children a world safer than the one we inhabit: a world not subject to nuclear blackmail or coercion, a world not frightened by insidious terrorist acts and not threatened by imbalances in the equilibrium of nature. Nor is this the only desire we share. There is, I know, still another: that in years to come we will be able to face our children and assure them that we did not lack the courage to face these difficult questions, did not lack the stamina to pursue the correct solutions.

In the past several months I have argued the importance of a strengthened safeguards regime with some 40 heads of government.... Senior government officials have travelled tens of thousands of miles in an effort to tighten existing safeguards and to broaden both the scope of their impact and the breadth of their application by supplier countries. We have raised the standard of our safeguards — with full support for the International Atomic Energy Agency which administers them — to the point that they are the toughest in the world. (And we are constantly on the alert for ways to make them more practical, more effective.) We impose as well still another constraint: we refuse to engage in nuclear co-operation without an explicit exclusion of explosive uses.

I do not pretend that the present international regime for the inspection and detection of nuclear cheating is foolproof. I am painfully aware that the N.P.T. is yet far from universally supported. I am deeply conscious of the responsibilities which devolve upon Canada as a world leader in the peaceful application of nuclear energy....

---

* Nuclear Non-Proliferation Treaty.

Chapter 2
The Strategy of "Nuclear Suffocation"

INTRODUCTION

*C*anadian concern about the proliferation of nuclear weapons, just described, was not limited to so-called "horizontal proliferation" — their spread to countries which did not have them — but also to "vertical proliferation." This term refers to the development of different sizes and types of weapons, to be used by nuclear powers from the local battlefield to the intercontinental mass launch.

In a 1978 speech to the first United Nations Special Session on Disarmament, Mr. Trudeau set out the concept of "nuclear suffocation" (pp. 27–36). He proposed that new developments should be stopped in the laboratory. Then at least the destabilizing emergence of entirely new systems with the potential, no matter how short-lived, to confer real or perceived advantage would be ended. Nuclear powers would be limited to refining their current weapons systems. The "oxygen" on which the arms race feeds would be cut off.

Nuclear suffocation is among the most novel and complete of the arms control strategies advanced by Mr. Trudeau. Although, as he said himself, the specific actions to be taken were frequently raised in the process of negotiations, the overall concept had a unique clarity and sense of purpose. The more diverse proposals which comprised the later "peace initiative" were chosen for their relative familiarity; the strategy of suffocation enunciated in 1978 was carried forward and further detailed in 1983–84.

Suffocation was, Mr. Trudeau admitted, a second-best approach. It recognized that arms control negotiations on existing weapons systems were highly complex and that complete disarmament was probably unattainable in the near future. But it was an attempt to salvage what remained of détente, already frayed by U.S. suspicion that the Soviet Union was using a relaxation of tensions to meddle in neutral countries and to stockpile nuclear weapons.

While the strategy of suffocation was a clean and, in several ways, brilliant concept, it did not draw a warm response from those expected to use their weapons with murderous intent. This lack of response probably accounts for the limited presentation which the Prime Minister made to the NATO Summit in

Washington four days after his United Nations address (pp. 37–38). To Mr. Trudeau's critics, nuclear suffocation was a "flash in the pan." But to paraphrase Winston Churchill's famous remark to the Canadian Parliament: "some flash, some pan."*

---

* Mr. Churchill was responding to Hitler's boast that he would wring the neck of the British Empire; he said, "some chicken, some neck."

SPEECH BY PIERRE ELLIOTT TRUDEAU, PRIME MINISTER OF CANADA, TO THE UNITED NATIONS GENERAL ASSEMBLY SPECIAL SESSION ON DISARMAMENT*

NEW YORK, MAY 26, 1978

Canada takes its place in a world discussion on disarmament as an industrial country, geographically placed between two heavily armed superpowers, with an obvious stake in the prevention of war in a nuclear age.

We are a member of a regional defensive alliance that includes three of the five nuclear weapons states. We are nonetheless a country that has renounced the production of nuclear weapons or the acquisition of such weapons under our control.

We have withdrawn from any nuclear role by Canada's Armed Forces in Europe and are now in the process of replacing with conventionally armed aircraft the nuclear-capable planes assigned to our forces in North America. We were thus not only the first country in the world with the capacity to produce nuclear weapons that chose not to do so, we are also the first nuclear armed country to have chosen to divest itself of nuclear weapons.

We have not, for more than a decade, permitted Canadian uranium to be used for military purposes by any country. We are a country that maintains strict controls over exports of military equipment and does not export any to areas of tension or actual conflict. We are, on the other hand, a major source of nuclear material, equipment, and technology for peaceful purposes.

My excuse for reciting these facts is that it has been an assumption of our policy that countries like Canada can do something to slow down the arms race. But, obviously, we can do a great deal more if we act together. That is why a great responsibility rests upon this special session.

It is not the business of this session to negotiate agreements. That will be the task of others. What we are here to do is to take stock and to prescribe. High expectations are focused on our deliberations in all our countries. To do justice to these expectations we must impart a fresh momentum to the lagging process of disarmament. The time for doing so could not be more opportune.

One of the most important instruments of arms control we have been able to put in place is the Non-Proliferation Treaty. It is also one of the most fragile because any party may withdraw from it on three months' notice. The Treaty reflects a delicate balance of undertakings. Many non-nuclear weapons states regard it as an unequal treaty. It is all the more important for the nuclear weapons states to strengthen confidence in the treaty. The best way to do so is to take early and effective steps to bring the nuclear arms race to halt. That is the undertaking the nuclear weapons states assumed when they signed the Treaty.

Non-proliferation is not the only dimension of the international system that is put at risk by an unrelenting arms race. Détente also is in danger. The dominant premise of a policy of détente is confidence. That is how it is defined in the Final Act to which thirty-five heads of state and government subscribed

---

*Parts of this speech originally delivered in French; here translated into English.

in Helsinki in 1975. Only in a climate of confidence will it be possible, over time, to transcend the realities of divergent ideologies and to fashion the links of a co-operation based on common interests and concerns. The arms race cuts across these purposes. The development of each new weapons system carries the risk of unbalancing the existing security equation. A policy of political détente, which has to be based on confidence, cannot be expected to withstand such strains indefinitely.

The arms race also defies the logic of an interdependent world. It is hardly credible that nations which have learned that their destinies are linked, that national aims can no longer be wholly realized within national boundaries, that beggaring our neighbours is the surest way of beggaring ourselves, should have discovered no better alternative to maintaining their security than an escalating balance of terror. And it is even less credible that, in a world of finite resources and in so many parts of which basic human needs remain unsatisfied, nearly $400 billion in resources should have to be spent year by year for purposes of security.

Security, even absolute security, is not an end in itself. It is only the setting that permits us to pursue our real ends: economic well-being, cultural attainment, the fulfilment of the human personality. But those ends are all incompatible with a world of neighbours armed to the teeth.

On all these counts, we are right in having chosen this moment in time to pause and survey the disarmament scene. What we face is a general tendency to add to arsenals as the only way of correcting perceived imbalances in security. That way lies the logic of the arms spiral. We must recognize it for what it is: a search for security, however elusive. And we must deal with it on its own terms. To attempt to divorce disarmament from security is to be left only with the bare bones of rhetoric.

ACHIEVING SECURITY THROUGH DISARMAMENT

How to achieve security through disarmament is the theme of the great debate that has been waged through much of the present century. . . . The terms of the debate have been drastically altered in the last twenty-five years by two developments. One was the advent of nuclear weapons, which has forced us to assimilate the concept of unusable power. The other was the transformation of the political map, which has brought a whole host of new international actors into the disarmament debate. Perhaps it is useful, nonetheless, to review the principal strands of the historic debate to see what relevance they may have for our efforts. . . .

The broad spectrum of proposals to achieve greater world stability and the reduction of tensions ranges all the way from what is sometimes called the "declaratory approach" to the notion of general and complete disarmament.

The declaratory approach encompasses the whole complex of non-aggression pacts, treaties of guarantee, security assurances, and bans on the use of certain weapons. The classic example . . . was the Kellogg-Briand Pact of 1928. The parties to it, which included all the major powers of the time, renounced war as an instrument of national policy and pledged themselves to settle disputes by peaceful means only. The Pact was regarded as the portent of a new era. The more devastating judgement of historians is that it clouded the vision of the statesmen of the nineteen-thirties.

The declaratory approach is not dead. It is implicit in the idea of a commitment to non-first use of nuclear weapons. That idea is being seriously advanced by some and seriously entertained by others. It is difficult to dismiss because it would give expression and authority to a widely shared perception of international morality.

It may have a part to play as an assurance to countries that have renounced nuclear weapons. But it is important not to mistake the shadow for the substance. Declarations of good intent are no substitute for real disarmament. They need be violated only once. At that point, they become scraps of paper. They have no impact on capabilities nor on the resources those capabilities consume. Indeed, their effect may be negative by diverting attention from the requirement of real disarmament, which is to reduce armed forces and armaments.

If the declaratory speech places an unreasonable reliance on the value of good intentions, the notion of general and complete disarmament has proved to be equally unrealistic in its expectations. The term was coined at the World Disarmament Conference in 1932. But the notion was at the heart of the Covenant of the League of Nations. The Covenant spoke of the "reduction of national armaments to the lowest point consistent with national safety."

The perspective shifted with the coming into being of the United Nations. With the experience of the Second World War still fresh in mind, the emphasis of the Charter was on collective security. With the development of nuclear weapons and the failure of the ideas embodied in the Charter, general and complete disarmament again emerged as the dominant theme in the disarmament debate. It has since been reaffirmed in countless resolutions as the basic principle and ultimate goal of the world community.

It is important to remember how wide a range of vision was embraced by the concept of general and complete disarmament in the early nineteen-sixties. What was envisaged was not only the disbanding of armed forces, the dismantling of military establishments, the cessation of weapons production, and the elimination of weapons stockpiles. The counterpart of global demilitarization was a global security system involving reliable procedures for the peaceful settlement of disputes and effective arrangements for the maintenance of peace in accordance with the principles of the Charter.

The vision is not to be faulted. General and complete disarmament remains the ultimate goal of our efforts to advance the reality of disarmament. In practice, it raised serious questions in the minds of the negotiators: what should be the military balance at each stage of the process?; what kind of an inspection system could be relied upon to give assurance that engagements were being carried out?; how would an international disarmament organization be composed and with what powers would it be invested?; what would be the shape of arrangements for keeping the peace in a disarmed world? In sum, what would be the impact of this ambitious concept on the security, not to speak of the sovereignty, of the parties at the end of the day?

In the fullness of time, we have to find answers to these questions. But the fact remains that the answers have so far eluded us. It was natural, therefore, that we should have lowered our sights to the more practical aim of making progress toward a disarmed world by building it brick by brick.

This is the course we have pursued over the past decade or so. Over that period, we have managed to negotiate a number of instruments on arms control on which we can look back as useful milestones in the construction of an international security system. As a result, the deployment of nuclear weapons on the seabed and in outer space has been precluded; biological weapons have been prohibited; environmental warfare has been outlawed in large measure; agreements have been reached to ban nuclear tests in all environments except underground, and to halt the proliferation of nuclear weapons to countries not yet possessing them. These are not negligible measures, even though all militarily significant states have not yet adhered to them.

Such measures as we have taken are sometimes described as peripheral. I believe that to call them peripheral is seriously to underrate them. They are a great advance over declarations of intention because they deal with capabilities and they are, therefore, verifiable, which intentions are not. They have an effect on the arms race by closing off certain options. It is true that the measures taken so far have foreclosed options that were, in large part, hypothetical. But they do set the stage for an attack on the heart of the arms race, which is how to foreclose options that are real and, in the absence of restraint, inescapable.

THE NUCLEAR ARMS RACE

Against this background, let me turn to the nuclear arms race. The preservation of peace and security between the nuclear powers and their allies today rests primarily on the mutual balance of deterrence. Simply put, that balance means that any act of nuclear war by either would be incalculable folly. Nevertheless, the apparent success so far of this system in preventing a global war should not close our minds to the problems it raises.

What particularly concerns me is the technological impulse that continues to lie behind the development of strategic nuclear weaponry. It is, after all, in the laboratories that the nuclear arms race begins.

The new technologies can require a decade or more to take a weapons system from research and development to production and eventual deployment. What this means is that national policies are pre-empted for long periods ahead. It also complicates the task of the foreign policy-maker because of the difficulty of inferring current intentions from military postures that may be the result of decisions taken a decade earlier. Thus, however much governments declare that they intend to pursue a policy of peace, their declarations cannot help but be called into question: for they have allowed the blind and unchecked momentum of the arms race to create and to put at their disposal military capabilities of an order of magnitude that other governments cannot prudently ignore.

In such a situation, there is a risk that foreign policy can become the servant of defence policy, which is not the natural order of policy-making.

There is also a high risk that new weapons systems will revive concerns about a disarming first-strike capability; or that they will tend to blur the difference between nuclear and conventional warfare; or that they will increase problems of verification.

All this suggests that stable deterrence remains an inadequate concept . . . a poor substitute for genuine world security.

These dangers have been perceived by both major nuclear powers. I believe that both are serious in wanting to arrest the momentum of the nuclear arms race. They have been engaged in a dialogue on strategic arms limitations for several years. The dialogue has produced some useful quantitative limits and others are under negotiation. But the process is painstaking and as I have watched it, with a full appreciation of its importance to the security interests of my own country, I have wondered whether there may not be additional concepts that could usefully be applied to it.

The negotiations under way between the major nuclear powers have shown that it is possible to confirm or codify an existing balance of forces. But they have also shown how difficult it is to go beyond that and to cut back on weapons systems once they have been developed and deployed. That is not only because they are there and invested interests have been created in their deployment. It is also because it has proven immensely complex to achieve the magic formula of equal security by placing limits on what are often quite disparate weapons systems.

The conclusion I have reached is that the best way of arresting the dynamic of the nuclear arms race may be by a strategy of "suffocation," by depriving the arms race of the oxygen on which it feeds. This could be done by a combination of four measures. Individually, each of these measures has been part of the arms control dialogue for many years. It is in their combination that I see ... a more coherent, a more efficient, and a more promising approach to curbing the nuclear arms race. The measures I have in mind are:

First, a comprehensive test ban to impede the further development of nuclear explosive devices. Such a ban is currently under negotiation. It has long been Canada's highest priority. I am pleased that the efforts of Canada's representatives and those of other countries stand a good chance of success during 1978. The computer can simulate testing conditions up to a point. But there is no doubt in my mind that a total test ban will represent a real qualitative constraint on weapons development.

Second, an agreement to stop the flight-testing of all new strategic delivery vehicles. This would complement the ban on the testing of warheads. I am satisfied that, in the present state of the art, such an agreement can be monitored, as it must be, by national technical means.

Third, an agreement to prohibit all production of fissionable material for weapons purposes. The effect of this would be to set a finite limit on the availability of nuclear weapons material. Such an agreement would have to be backed up by an effective system of full-[scope] safeguards. It would have the great advantage of placing nuclear weapons states on a much more comparable basis with non-nuclear weapons states than they have been thus far under the dispensations of the Non-Proliferation Treaty.

Fourth, an agreement to limit and then progressively to reduce military spending on new strategic nuclear weapons systems. This will require the development of the necessary openness in reporting, comparing, and verifying such expenditures.

It is arguable that the credibility of such an agreement could be strengthened by placing the sums released from national accounts on international deposit, at least for an interim period, possibly in the form of special loans to international development institutions. Such an idea would be in line with conventional thinking about what should be done with at least some of the savings from disarmament. But I do not think it makes good sense to penalize countries that act responsibly by cutting back on armaments....

A strategy of suffocation seems to me to have a number of advantages. It is not merely declaratory because it will have a real and progressive impact on the development of new strategic weapons systems. It will have that impact in three ways: by freezing the available amount of fissionable material; by preventing any technology that may be developed in the laboratory from being tested; and by reducing the moneys devoted to military expenditure. It is also a realistic strategy because it assumes that, for some time to come at least, total nuclear disarmament is probably unattainable in practice. It avoids some of the problems encountered in the negotiations currently under way in that it does not involve complex calculations of balance but leaves the nuclear weapons states some flexibility in adjusting their existing weapons technology. It has at least the potential of reducing the risks of conflict that are inherent in the technological momentum of strategic competition.

The ultimate intent of a strategy of suffocation is to halt the arms race in the laboratory. But an offer to halt the arms at any stage is also a step in the direction of genuine disarmament. The President of the United States has shown the way... with his far-sighted postponement of a decision to produce a special battlefield nuclear weapon. We must all hope that the response of the Soviet Union will be such as to make it possible to extend that postponement indefinitely.

NON-PROLIFERATION

So much for the vertical dimension of the nuclear problem. Let me now say a word about the horizontal spread of nuclear capabilities.

There are those who have a fatalistic view of the proliferation of nuclear weapons. They argue that nuclear proliferation is ultimately unavoidable and that there is little sense in putting undue constraints on the international flow of nuclear energy resources.

I do not share that view. I note with satisfaction that the list of countries said to be on the verge of a nuclear weapons capability is not very different today from what it was a decade or so ago. I believe world security would be seriously diminished by the further spread of nuclear weapons and that it is the responsible course for governments to pursue policies based on the presumption that proliferation can be stopped.

We in Canada have perhaps gone further in our support for an effective non-proliferation system than have most other countries. In part, this is the result of national experience. But in much larger part, it is a reflection of public opinion in Canada which does not believe that we would be serving the cause of a rational world order by being negligent in the requirements we place on Canadian nuclear exports.

I make no apology for Canada's precedent-setting safeguards policy, though it has been criticized by some as being too stringent. Canada is asking of others no more than what we have ourselves accepted voluntarily as a party to the Non-Proliferation Treaty. We have not manipulated our safeguards for commercial advantage, nor have we hesitated to accept commercial loss where our safeguards have inhibited nuclear sales. We have shared our technology freely with developing countries and we have applied our safeguards to all on a non-discriminatory basis and without trying to distinguish between capability and intention.

Canada judged it necessary to adopt a national policy, even though nuclear transfers were already within the compass of international regulation. Canadian action was based on genuine concern about our role as a nuclear supplier. We did not think that the international safeguards system, as it stood, was likely to be equal to the problems posed by the advance of nuclear technology. Our object was to bring about a new, more effective international consensus....

[T]he international system will need time to adapt to the new energy situation.* It is now accepted by all that nuclear energy will have to play an increasing part in meeting incremental world energy needs in the remainder of the century. It is equally accepted that the benefits of nuclear energy must be accessible to all countries having no alternative energy options.

It is understandable that, with the experience of another energy crisis still fresh in their minds, many countries would like to aim at a high degree of energy independence. In particular, they will expect to be protected against the interruption, without due cause, of essential supplies of nuclear fuel. Any new system will need to accommodate these aspirations.

But we shall also have to consider that we are hovering on the threshold of a plutonium economy. We shall have to make sure that the vulnerable points in the fuel cycle are capable of being adequately safeguarded by technical means... [or by] institutional arrangements for international management. [I]n the end, the best prospect for countries to assure their national energy security lies in an international system that carries the confidence of nuclear suppliers.

There are limits to the contribution that can be made by nations acting unilaterally. I believe that Canada's efforts to date have been constructive and effective. But further achievement can be made only through multilateral agreement. We intend to play our full part in the working out of the assurances and the constraints that will inevitably have to form part of an enhanced international system of non-proliferation.

While nuclear proliferation remains a source of concern, it has shown itself amenable to control. That is more than can yet be said about the transfer of conventional weapons.

CONVENTIONAL RESTRAINT

The problem of conventional weapons is serious.... Conventional weapons are the germs of a highly contagious disease. Eighty percent of the world's military expenditures are accounted for by developing countries. Well over half of the developing countries devote at least ten percent of their public spending to military purposes; nearly a quarter of them spend in excess of twenty-five percent. It is with conventional weapons that 133 wars have been fought since 1945, involving 80 countries and killing 25 million people.

Meanwhile the transfer of conventional weapons is assuming massive proportions; in the aggregate some $20 billion is being expended on it each year. There can be no first and second priorities, therefore, as between the nuclear and a whole series of conventional arms races. Both are relevant to the maintenance of world security; both are absorbing resources better devoted to other purposes; both are the legitimate business of an organization whose purpose it is to harmonize the actions of nations.

The traffic in conventional arms involves producers, consumers, and the transactions between them. What can we do about it?

The more closely we look at the problem, the more clearly we can see that the question of sales is not easily divorced from... production. The production

---

* A reference to the OPEC oil price increase of 1973 and subsequent energy policy changes.

of military equipment is attractive for countries with an appropriate industrial base and with requirements of such equipment for their own armed forces. It contributes to national security; it reduces external payments; it creates jobs. Moreover, the attraction of production for defence is enhanced by the fact that some seventy percent of new technology today derives from the military and space sectors.

The problem is that the more states go into the production of weapons to meet their own security needs, the more tempting it is for them to try to achieve lower unit costs and other economic benefits by extending their production runs and selling such weapons abroad. Almost every country that produces some military equipment finds itself, to a greater or lesser degree, caught on the horns of this dilemma. My country is no exception.

Of course, any particular country intent on making a contribution to world security could decide to abstain from producing arms. But what significance would such a gesture actually have? So long as arms are being bought, arms will be produced. There is no particular moral merit in a country that is buying arms not producing them. And if the main reason for not producing them is not to be involved in selling them, it will have no practical impact on the arms race because other suppliers will readily fill the gap.

One way out of this dilemma would be for suppliers, acting in concert, to practise restraint. That is easier where the incentive for arms sales is mainly commercial. It is more difficult where considerations of foreign policy are involved. Canada is not an important exporter of military equipment. We account for about one percent of world sales. We could accept any consensus that may be arrived at among suppliers to cut back on military exports. We recognize that our position differs from that of others.

The major powers, in particular, sometimes see arms sales as a means of maintaining a balance of confidence in situations where political solutions continue to elude the parties. But the major powers must also recognize that a balance of confidence can be achieved in such situations at lower levels of cost and risk. I welcome the recent decision of the United States and the Soviet Union to look for a basis of mutual restraint in their sales of conventional weapons.

Restraint by suppliers will help. But it is an incomplete answer to the arms traffic problem. It may also cause resentment among potential arms purchasers. For better or for worse, much of the arms traffic takes place between industrialized and developing countries. The purchasing countries seek, as is their right, to ensure their own security. In many cases, they seek no more than to maintain law and order on their national soil. To curb their right to acquire arms by purchase, even to place qualitative restraints on such purchases, would revive much of the acrimony of the North-South dialectic. It would be regarded, rightly or wrongly, as another instance where the rich are trying to substitute their judgement for that of the poor. Moreover, attempts to curb the transfer of conventional weapons would do nothing to change the incentive for acquiring them.

It is at the level of incentives that we are likely to manage best to come to grips with the problem of conventional weapons. The incentive to acquire arms is rooted in apprehensions of insecurity. The best way to allay such apprehensions is through collective regional arrangements. The countries of Latin America have set the world a useful example in turning their continent into a nuclear weapons-free zone and in persuading outside powers to respect that status. Similar arrangements are conceivable, in Latin America as elsewhere, to deal with the acquisition of conventional arms. It would be for regional decision-makers to devise incentives for restraint and sanctions for excess in the accumulation of conventional arsenals and in the build-up of conventional forces. That, in the long run, seems to me the best prospect of curbing the conventional arms race without damage to the relations between nations.

PEACEKEEPING AND SECURITY

While we are exploring these and other ways of making progress on disarmament, we must also strengthen our joint capacity to maintain international peace and security. Substantive progress on disarmament is at best a matter of years, if not of decades. Meanwhile the security of nations is bound to remain precarious.

In a world of a hundred and fifty or more states, many of which have claims upon their neighbours, and where resource shortages and population movements raise questions of life and death for millions of people, violence within and between states is a regrettable fact of life.

The United Nations was created to restrain and, if possible, to prevent war. Its record is a mixed one. But whatever we may think of its capacities, we must work as best we can to improve and to strengthen them. Recent events have demonstrated once again both the uncertainties of peacekeeping operations and the continuing need to make these operations a success. It must be our objective to create the conditions that will permit all members to respond quickly, impartially, and effectively to threats to peace whenever they are called upon by the United Nations to do so. I make this plea on behalf of a country that has made peacekeeping a special plank in its defence policy and has participated in every major peacekeeping operation in the United Nations....

Proposals have also been made to strengthen the capacity of the United Nations for research on disarmament matters and to make the results of such research more widely available. We welcome proposals of this kind. In this as in other matters of public policy, governments can only benefit from more informed discussion. Disarmament is the business of everyone but only a few are able to follow the issues. The consequence is that special interests dominate the debate and distort the conclusions. We must make sure that they do not carry the day. Dispassionate research and analysis, presented in terms that people can understand, would do much to right the balance....

As long ago as 1929, that most eloquent of advocates of disarmament, Salvador de Madriaga, spoke of disarmament as being "really the problem of the organization of the world community." In the larger sense of the word, history has proved him right. The arms race we are here to stop is a symptom of the insecurity of nations. But it is more than that. It is a latent source of world catastrophe.

That is why this special session has been called together. It is the first major assize on disarmament to have been held since the end of the Second World War. We must not allow the opportunity to pass without putting our imprint on the course of events. We cannot expect to settle all the issues in our deliberations. We shall certainly not settle them by producing paper.

What we must try to achieve is a reasonable consensus on broad objectives and on a plan of action for the next few years. If we can do that, if we can hold out hope that the arms race can be reversed, we will have taken a significant step toward the better ordering of the affairs of our planet.

STATEMENT BY PRIME MINISTER TRUDEAU AT THE NATO SUMMIT

WASHINGTON, D.C., MAY 30, 1978

What is the situation that confronts us on the other side [of the East-West divide]? The [NATO] study of long term trends in East-West relations holds out little prospect of significant change in the Soviet Union. That is perhaps too conservative a conclusion. But we must probably accept that what change may come about will not be such as radically to alter the calculations about Western security that we have had to make over the past generation.

The Soviet Union will continue to regard the USA as the only power capable of fundamentally challenging Soviet security, which means that it will continue to attempt to match the USA as a global power with power globally deployable. It will also, presumably, continue to assess the other combined threats to Soviet security, including the desire to preserve its paramountcy in Eastern Europe, as requiring a military posture that we in the West regard as being excessive based on any reasonable assumptions. As has been said by a seasoned observer of the Soviet scene, the Soviet Union is unlikely ever to feel secure except in circumstances where everyone else feels insecure.

We have received repeated assurances from Soviet leaders that their massive military capacity neither threatens nor is intended to threaten our security. We should note these assurances and weigh them carefully. They are not without importance or value. But it would be imprudent if we were to base our policies on assurances rather than actions — on declared or assumed intentions rather than on manifest capabilities. We cannot wait for the Soviet Union to develop such a preponderance of military capability that the balance will swing strongly in its favour, enabling it to achieve security on its own terms. The Soviet Union's assurance of complete security cannot be bought at the cost of our incapacity to protect ourselves. That would be no basis either for security or for détente. In seeking to improve the reality of our security, we must maintain the balance of deterrent strength. But our security problem will not be solved simply by the reactive policy of trying to match the military capacity of the potential adversary. We must also pursue with vigour, at every opportunity and along every avenue open to us, the goals of a meaningful policy of détente and a genuine reduction in our mutual capacity to wage war.

In the long run, there is no real alternative to pursuing détente with the Soviet Union — a process which we must continue to promote. But, for détente to be pursued and made a permanent feature of the East-West relationship, confidence must exist not only between governments. It must exist also between and among our citizens for, in the West, it is our publics that determine how fast and in what direction we can proceed. This public confidence can only be maintained if the human dimension of détente, as embodied in the Helsinki Final Act, is respected and the individual is allowed his rightful place in society and in contacts across frontiers. If détente is seen to be applied selectively, support for it is likely to erode. This prospect cannot be treated lightly by any government.

I attended the Special Session on Disarmament of the United Nations only a few days ago. While arms control and disarmament are sometimes obscured by controversy and diverted by rhetoric, I believe there is today a real and widespread yearning for a turning of the corner — for a reversal of the arms race and a real concern about where present trends will lead us. This presents NATO with both an opportunity and a challenge to find ways in which security can be achieved at lower levels of armament. The search for security can too easily be conducted only through armaments improvement. It must also be sought through effective arms control and disarmament. The members of the Alliance should undertake a major effort to develop further positive and constructive proposals in this domain . . . .

The value of NATO's consultative mechanisms are nowhere better illustrated than in the immense variety of questions involved in East-West relations. Members of the Alliance have long recognized that collective security is best guaranteed by a combined pursuit of an adequate defence capability and of a general climate of confidence and mutual respect in the broad spectrum of relationships between East and West. Canda and other NATO members are working individually and collectively to achieve that goal through their commitment to a policy of détente.

It is fitting . . . to recall the creative role played by Canadians in the building of NATO, beginning with Prime Minister Louis St. Laurent's original formulation of the fundamental concept of the Alliance in the House of Commons on April 28, 1948. This founding vision of NATO has served us well for thirty years and will continue to guide us in an ever-changing world.

Chapter 3

Better Communications between the Superpowers

INTRODUCTION

*F*ollowing the Soviet invasion of Afghanistan in 1979, the already crumbling spirit of détente between East and West dissipated rapidly. The Carter Administration became totally absorbed in the Iranian hostage crisis and the will to move further on arms control or other fronts was lost. The election of President Ronald Reagan in November 1980 brought to power a man with long-standing ideological views on the Soviet Union; he expressed those views to domestic audiences, whatever the international consequences. As Mr. Trudeau said in his convocation speech at Notre Dame University (pp. 40–43), "each side is acting in ways which the other perceives to be threatening." In the Soviet case, it was by the invasion of Afghanistan and threats against Poland. In the American case, it was by references to "an evil empire," and in March 1983, announcement of the "Strategic Defence Initiative."

After raising the problem of growing suspicion in May 1982, Mr. Trudeau sought to build upon his "suffocation" proposals at the second United Nations Special Session on Disarmament in June (pp. 44–48). In particular, he proposed a ban on all weapons for use in outer space, a concept carried forward into the peace initiative as a ban on high-altitude anti-satellite weapons.

He argued strongly, and with some success, at least on paper, that the Williamsburg Seven Nations Summit should recommit the leadership of the West to "serious arms control negotiations" (p. 49).

In addition, he engaged in a domestic debate with critics of the Canadian Government's commitment to test the guidance system for the Cruise missile. Although he sought to convey his respect for critics' views and their right to protest (as he had done himself two decades earlier), he stood his ground. He wrote an open letter to the Canadian public and then discussed the topic further in press interviews (pp. 50–54).

But the Canadian Government recognized that demonstrations of alliance solidarity, namely the testing of the Cruise, did not necessarily prompt greater readiness by the Americans on arms control matters. This recognition led to the tentative thoughts which became the Trudeau "peace initiative" of 1983–84.

TRANSCRIPT OF REMARKS BY THE PRIME MINISTER AT THE CONVOCATION CEREMONY, NOTRE DAME UNIVERSITY

SOUTH BEND, INDIANA, MAY 16, 1982

...Joyful moments are too often dampened by solemn speakers. What I have to say today will certainly be sober stuff, but it will not be unrelieved gloom. Oliver Edwards earned immortality when he said to Samuel Johnson: "You are a philosopher, Dr. Johnson. I have tried too in my time to be a philosopher; but, I don't know how, cheerfulness was always breaking in." For my part...I am a realist but, somehow, optimism always keeps breaking out.

Occasions such as this, by their very design, are intended to place our lives in perspective. As does each one of you, I regard the future with a mixture of excitement and apprehension. Humanity is confronted with formidable challenges. Governments are perplexed in the face of those challenges.

Our times are "interesting," as the Chinese might say, not only due to the sagging health of the industrialized societies but also because of the menacing confrontation between the two superpowers and the simple, terrible fear that we all could be caught up in a thermonuclear exchange.

Even among the members of the North Atlantic Alliance, we must contend with consistent strains that threaten our unity: the invasion of Afghanistan, martial law in Poland, turmoil in Central America. We perceive a growing and disturbing divergence of views between Europe and North America, and a belief that economic and military burdens are unequally shared.

In the face of such uncertainty, our people are growing more apprehensive and more critical — more critical of their institutions and their leaders. Once again, people are taking to the streets in significant numbers to express their frustration and calling for measures that others in turn believe will only worsen the situation.

The United States has a special role to play in this dangerously disturbed and divided world; a role based on power and the responsible use of it. Superpower, to be more precise, and super-responsibility. This burden places upon Americans an enormous weight, and it is not surprising that you have known moments of self-doubt and withdrawal. The health and vitality of our system and way of life is, ultimately, in your hands.

Our strength lies in our easy understanding of each other. We, your friends and allies, recognize that some decisions, only the United States can take; equally, however, there are decisions that require consultation and a sharing of responsibilities....

As a superpower, the United States has the responsibility of leadership and the means to exercise it. As allies, we have a duty not only to support your leadership but also to ensure that your actions take account of the legitimate goals of the other members of the Alliance. As friends, we have a duty to hold up the looking glass in which you see yourselves.

So, I want today to discharge one of my responsibilities and hold up the looking glass for a short while. I want to speak about the need for greater understanding between East and West.

The mood of confrontation that exists today has given rise to an unprecedented level of public anxiety. Our fears are rooted in the perception that both sides may be prepared to contemplate using the ultimate weapon in order to achieve pre-eminence. We are worried by the deployment of SS-20s in Eastern Europe. But we are also worried about statements in the United States about the "survivability" of nuclear war, about "demonstration explosions" and first strike scenarios.

The two sides are increasingly isolated from each other. Scoring propaganda points has become more important than improving understanding. Each side is acting in ways which the other perceives to be threatening. There is a widening gulf of suspicion between East and West, and there is concern that we are finding ourselves in the midst of an ever-accelerating arms race.

The key to bridging this gulf lies not simply in armament or disarmament, nor in the numbers of nuclear warheads in the respective arsenals. It is to be found instead in the concept of security. Nations arm out of fear for their security and will disarm only if they are convinced that the threat to their security has diminished.

In their last conflict with a Western power, the Soviets suffered the loss of some 20 million people. Perhaps because of their experience, the U.S.S.R. harbours concepts of security that leave the rest of us feeling insecure. Even if one agrees that the Soviet divisions in Eastern Europe are not in place to threaten the West but rather as a check against internal dissent — a guarantee of Soviet hegemony — the fact remains that four million Warsaw Pact troops do pose a potential threat to Western Europe. We the West, being unwilling to match their forces with equal armies of our own, must rely on nuclear forces to offset them.

This, in turn, is not very reassuring to the Soviets. In much the same way that conventional forces in Eastern Europe pose a potential threat to Western Europe, our nuclear deterrent force is surely seen by them as potentially aggressive.

In recent years there have been many efforts to improve East-West security. In 1978, I enunciated a "strategy of suffocation." Since it takes years of research and testing to bring into use new instruments of destruction, in essence, my strategy called for the suppression of these developments in the laboratory. This was never intended to mean that any country should unilaterally pursue this strategy. For it to be workable, it entails multilateral agreement to bring it into effect.

In the absence of a positive response from any quarter, the Canadian Government subsequently endorsed NATO's "two-track" approach — seeking to improve our defensive position by preparing to introduce new intermediate-range weapons in Europe, while at the same time pursuing arms reduction negotiations.... Canada, despite considerable domestic pressure, undertook to negotiate an agreement allowing the testing of Cruise missiles in our territory.

It is a sad reflection on the difficulties inherent in arms reductions that there had to be progress along the track which leads to the introduction of new weapons before movement could begin along the negotiating track.

Clearly, the key to achieving meaningful Soviet participation in arms reduction schemes will lie in demonstrating ways in which they will benefit them. What is needed is more than mere bookkeeping and auditing. We must also convince each other that our intentions are what we say they are.

This cannot be done by isolating ourselves or isolating the Soviets on every political, social, and economic issue. We must speak to each other, not just occasionally, and not just between leaders. In short, we must recognize that the

U.S.S.R. is a superpower; that it has strategic interests and the might to protect those interests. Only then will we be able to come up to a mutual understanding about the desirability of arms reductions.

When we set out to achieve that goal we will need to follow two guidelines.

First, a balance of forces is a necessary objective, but not a sufficient one. For if we reduce our arsenal considerably, to roughly equal strength, and then immediately turn around and make the rest of our arms faster, more accurate, and more difficult to detect, it will not take long to upset the balance.

Therefore, in this day of rapid technological advance, a mere balance, whether at a high level or moderate level, is inherently unstable. The real attraction in arms control lies not only in achieving a balance but in setting parameters within which balance can be verified and maintained.

Second, since the major source of pressure exercised by the Soviets on the global balance of power derives from their military strength, the West should negotiate arms control and disarmament with single-minded determination. The Soviets threaten us militarily; not culturally, not politically, and certainly not economically. Consequently, we should not seek to link non-military objectives with disarmament.

Any. . . attempt to impose our values on the other superpower or to settle other scores can only heighten their belief that we are not serious about peace.

There should be no debate about the paramount importance of bringing under control a threat to the human race.

There should be no question that such control requires communication and understanding between those who can exercise the threat.

Arms control is demonstrably a matter of mutual interest, and the contribution it makes to stability and survival should outweigh all other considerations.

I am not asking the superpowers to love each other or even to trust each other. Just to talk to each other because they have an equal interest in preventing the calamity that unfortunately has ceased to be unthinkable.

Happily, the improvements in technology offer possible solutions. Trust is no longer a sine qua non in achieving international stability. Methods of verification have become startlingly accurate.

It was the politicians who doubted the validity of the ill-fated SALT II treaty. Scientists, technicians, and military men were satisfied that, within acceptable limits, it was verifiable. With such treaties, confidence can improve to the point where more effective measures of verification can be contemplated. And if this means that we will eventually be led to inspect each other's laboratories, so much the better!

The long parade of eminent military and scientific personalities — in both camps — who have devoted their lives to perfecting systems of mass destruction and who now cry for an end to isolation and the beginning of dialogue are proof enough that the politicians had better start listening.

Many were deeply disappointed when your Congress failed to ratify the SALT II Treaty. We have not been greatly heartened by the results to date in the discussions of controls on intermediate-range weapons which began last November in Geneva.

For this reason, I welcome the prospect of a summit meeting between President Reagan and President Brezhnev. I am encouraged by President Reagan's announcement. . . that the United States proposes negotiations with the Soviet Union at the end of June on the reduction of strategic weapons. I welcome this *start*.

I am certain that these steps will reassure your friends and begin to restore cohesion to our Alliance.

Let us accept the challenge to take bold initiatives. Let us pledge that we will not be the ones to start a war. Let us again seek agreement to suffocate horrifying new weapons in the laboratory. Let us develop new approaches to arms control.

Americans, have confidence in your strength. You are strong in yourselves, and strong in your friends.

Strength dares! Let there be a new beginning in the relationship between East and West.

TRANSCRIPT OF THE PRIME MINISTER'S ADDRESS TO THE SECOND UNITED NATIONS SPECIAL SESSION ON DISARMAMENT*

NEW YORK, JUNE 18, 1982

The message Canada brings to this Assembly is not one of military strength or power. It is a message of peace which I bring you, a message which all countries, whether strong or weak, rich or poor, must make heard at the present time.

Only the deaf cannot hear the clamour arising all over the world against the arms race. In some countries, people's anguish and anger are freely expressed. In some others, people's voices are muffled by repression, but can still be heard by us.

In both cases, however, the message is clear. Men and women from every country are addressing a most urgent appeal to their leaders. They are telling us to seize the opportunity of the Special Session to start building a system capable of restraining the suicidal rivalry in which we are stuck.

As we contemplate the business at hand, we must remind ourselves that disarmament is not simply a technical matter; it cannot be isolated from the world context. If we want to know why so little progress has been made in the four years that have elapsed since our first Special Session, we can do no better than to cast our minds back to some of the events that have erupted on the world scene over that period — particularly recently — and to wonder what has happened to the Charter.... [T]he Charter is international law. In adopting it, each and every one of our countries has made it apart of our national law. The Charter lays down, as a prime requisite of world order, that "all members shall refrain in their international relations from the threat or use of force" in any manner inconsistent with the purposes of the United Nations.

The plea is made, from time to time, in favour of an undertaking of non-first use of nuclear weapons. I have no quarrel with those making the plea, who are serious persons concerned about the horrendous implications of the outbreak of nuclear warfare. However, the Charter lays down that there shall be no first use of force — any force. This law binds all of us....

But let us recognize that arguments about first use do not really go to the heart of the matter. The real problem before us is how to break the arms spiral. We will not do that in circumstances where any of the parties feels deficient in its security.... Arms control, to be viable, must increase security, not reduce it.

Security, unfortunately, is an elusive concept. It is not only a matter of weaponry. It is also a matter of perception. When each side acts in ways which the other perceives to be threatening, the gulf of suspicion widens between East and West.

But the shadow that overhangs all arms control negotiations, and has led to the unravelling of some, comes mainly from the fact that we are dealing with an array of very different weapons systems in circumstances where technological innovation tends to overtake a negotiation even while it is in progress.

---

*Parts of this speech, including the opening, were made in French, but here have been translated into English. Mr. Trudeau has slightly edited the speech.

I believe that we must reconcile ourselves to the notion that total security is not achievable for any country in today's world. An attempt to achieve it can only result in everyone else feeling insecure....

It has always been a useful precept of diplomatic negotiation that the outcome must take account of the legitimate interests of both sides. Arms control negotiations are no exception. An attempt by one side to make strategic gains at the expense of the other will not, in the end, work. Only measures that increase mutual security are likely to offer a way out of the present paralysis. In particular, the two superpowers must start with the recognition that each has strategic interests and the strength to protect those interests.

... The nuclear arms build-up is causing anguish to many people in many parts of the world. They are disturbed by the rehearsal of nuclear scenarios in a deteriorating political climate. They are posing their own questions about reasonable definitions of security. They are reminding political leaders that what is at stake is the crucial matter of the life or death of mankind.

As Prime Minister of a country that, from the outset, renounced a nuclear weapons capability of its own, I understand full well the people's anguish and confusion. The nuclear debate is difficult and seems to pursue an inverse logic. It deals with power that, by common consent, is unusable. It argues for more nuclear weapons in order that, in the end, there may be fewer. It perceives the vulnerability of cities and of human beings as an element of stability in the nuclear balance. And worst of all, the debate goes on without much evidence of any light at the end of the tunnel.

When we met in 1978, a dialogue on strategic arms limitations had been going on between the major nuclear powers for several years. A comprehensive nuclear test ban seemed on the verge of conclusion: it never was concluded. Subsequently, another negotiation — SALT II — was concluded: it has not been ratified.

I do not believe it would be productive at this time for the Assembly to try to apportion blame for those failures. I remain convinced that both the major nuclear powers are intent on dissipating the threat of nuclear confrontation.

In this regard, there are some positive developments. Negotiations to reduce intermediate-range nuclear forces began, as we know, late last year and, following President Reagan's Eureka initiative, the long-awaited talks on limiting and reducing strategic arms will resume [shortly]. All of us have an enormous stake in these negotiations; failure to reach an early satisfactory conclusion could have dramatic consequences. Let me illustrate this assertion.

Since the first Special Session [in 1978], a new generation of intermediate-range missiles has been deployed by the Soviet Union. Three hundred SS-20s now pose a threat to Western Europe. The Alliance to which Canada belongs has decided to counter the Soviet threat by deploying new Pershing II and ground-launched Cruise missiles; and at the same time to engage the U.S.S.R. in negotiations aimed at setting limits on the systems of both sides at the lowest possible level.

It follows that unless the negotiations accomplish their objective by late next year, new weapons of terror will be added to the NATO arsenal.* Having attended the [recent] NATO Summit meeting... I can testify that we passion-

---

* The negotiations were unsuccessful and the missiles *were* deployed.

ately want these negotiations to succeed in removing the current threat and thereby obviating the need to deploy new missiles of our own. But what will be the position of the Warsaw Pact countries? I must assume that they too will negotiate in good faith. I would add, however, that they would be ill-advised to assume that public demonstrations in the West will weaken our negotiating position.

True, hundreds of thousands of demonstrators in Western Europe, in Canada, and here in New York...have taken pains to express the extent to which a renewed arms race is fundamentally repugnant to their values. In many ways, I suppose most of us in this Assembly agree with them. That similar demonstrations have not taken place in Eastern Europe does not, I think, suggest that the people of the member countries of the Warsaw Pact are any more comfortable with the prospect of mutual incineration; rather, it may be due to the fact that they are denied not only the right to express publicly their views but, indeed, to acquire the knowledge and understanding on which such views might be founded. It would be a grave miscalculation were the Soviets to misinterpret the very strength of our democratic system as a demonstration of weakness of our resolve.

It is with considerable conviction, therefore, that I call on the INF negotiators to achieve real progress within the limited time remaining so that, in this instance, the armaments spiral will not be allowed to proceed to twist.

In seeking to arrest the arms race, the problem that continues to preoccupy me is the technological momentum that lies at its root. We must come to grips with that problem... [a] central point of my presentation to this assembly four years ago. Let me return to it briefly.

I start with the proposition that all new weapons systems are potentially destabilizing.... [S]uch systems will heighten concerns about a disarming first-strike capability, or will tend to blur the difference between nuclear and conventional warfare, or will increase the problems of verification.

Instability is the fuel that feeds the nuclear arms race. That is why...I put before this assembly a "strategy of suffocation" designed to deprive the nuclear arms race of the oxygen on which it feeds, from the laboratories to the testing sites.

The main elements of the strategy had long been familiar features of the arms control dialogue: a comprehensive test ban; a halt to the flight-testing of all new strategic delivery vehicles; a cessation of the production of fissionable material for weapons purposes; and a limitation, and eventual reduction, of military spending for new strategic weapons systems. It was in the *combination* of these elements that I saw a more coherent, a more efficient, and a more promising instrument for curbing the nuclear arms race.

But the strategy was never meant to be applied unilaterally. It always envisaged negotiated agreements between the nuclear powers. All elements of the strategy would probably not fall into place at once. But all were essential if the strategy were to have its full effect: the halt of the technological momentum of the arms race, by freezing at the testing stage the development of new weapons systems.

While I continue to believe that such a technological freeze is fundamental to controlling the arms race, I would now propose, however, that it be enfolded into a more general policy of *stabilization*.

I do not consider the strategy of suffocation to be in competition with current negotiations or with negotiations shortly to commence. [T]he more successful these negotiations are, the more likely will they need to be entrenched in agreements along the lines I have proposed.

The impact of the current and proposed negotiations, if they succeed, will be to produce a stable balance at a much lower level of armament. It will involve not only important quantitative reductions, but a qualitative change, in that destabilizing systems will have been reduced. . . .

Thus a policy of stabilization has two complementary components: the suffocation strategy which seeks to inhibit the development of new weapons systems, and our current negotiating approach aimed at qualitative and quantitative reductions in nuclear arsenals designed to achieve a stable balance at lower levels.

Before I leave the subject of suffocation, I must underscore the urgency of coming to grips with the development of new weaponry for use in outer space. Twenty-five years ago, the first man-made satellite was launched. That event marked a leap in man's mastery of the Earth's environment. Fifteen years ago, it did not seem premature to close off the possibility that space might be used for other than peaceful purposes. But today, the Treaty of Principles Governing the Activities of States in the Exploration and Use of Outer Space is patently inadequate. That is how quickly, in today's world, science fiction becomes reality.

The treaty lays down that nuclear or other weapons of mass destruction are not to be placed in orbit, around the earth, or stationed in space. In retrospect, that leaves loopholes which risk being highly destabilizing.

I am thinking particularly of anti-satellite weapons or anti-missile laser systems.* I believe that we cannot wait much longer if we are to be successful in foreclosing the prospect of space wars. I propose . . . that an early start be made on a treaty to prohibit the development, testing, and deployment of all weapons for use in outer space.

Of course, the whole edifice rests on key assumptions about verification, and it is to the theory and practice of verification that we must increasingly give attention.

Openness is central to the process of verification. But here, too, technology has taken us well beyond the notions about openness that were prevalent only twenty-five years ago. When we speak of verification by "national technical means," we have in mind the vast range of activity that is detectable by the magic eye of highly sophisticated satellites plying their intrusive orbits around the globe. I sometimes wonder whether we realize that a certain reluctance in accepting the rigours of verification is an insufferable anachronism.

Verification is not only a matter of access. Verification entails a technology of its own that differs from weapons system to weapons system. Therefore, ideally, the work on verification should prepare the way for arms control agreements that still lie ahead; otherwise, problems of verification will inevitably prevent the conclusion of even well-advanced arms control negotiations. In

---

*The latter now form an important option for the Strategic Defense Initiative. Mr. Trudeau's warning about their destabilizing potential was issued nine months before President Reagan's speech on the subject.

this context I am encouraged by the positive approach to verification procedures contained in the remarks of the Soviet Foreign Minister....*

However, given the complexity and characteristics of many modern weapons systems, so-called "national technical means" may not be adequate for verifying arms control or disarmament agreements. Consequently, the international community should address itself to verification as one of the most significant factors in disarmament negotiations in the 1980s.

In Canada, we are allocating increased funds for arms control and disarmament initiatives. This decision will allow us to take two important steps. First, we are committing resources to enable Canada to become a full participant in the international seismic data exchange, the international verification mechanism which will form a part of the provisions of a comprehensive test ban treaty. We believe that the exchange should be fully operational at an early date and in advance of the treaty. Secondly, we will substantially increase research in verification. To develop effective verification procedures, Canada will be devoting more attention to utilizing expertise available inside and outside government.

...In the course of this Session, many good proposals will have been put before us, including those in the Report of the Palme Commission, which has made a significant contribution to public awareness and understanding of the issues. I have tried, from a Canadian perspective, to make a number of precise proposals of my own, in the context of a policy of stabilization....

In the process of sifting the proposals before us, I hope that the Special Session will concentrate on what, with goodwill, is achievable. This Assembly has a right to expect sincerity of purpose and a determination to achieve concrete results on the part of all participants. A particularly heavy responsibility rests with the two superpowers. They must give their undivided attention to negotiations to reduce their arsenals of nuclear weapons and should not deviate from that central objective by imposing political preconditions.

This implies that the superpowers agree to communicate, to talk to each other, and to recognize the unquestionable common interest which unites them in a fundamental way; that is, the need to avoid a catastrophe which would destroy them both.†

When the security of the world and the fate of the human race are at stake, all governments have a duty to raise their voices on behalf of the societies they represent....

"The highest form of hope," said Bernanos, "is the overcoming of despair." That is what is demanded of us by the millions of men and women who are alarmed by the arms race and the prospect of a nuclear holocaust.

The most unpardonable failure of this assembly would be to kill, by inaction, the hope in people's hearts. For, in the face of the demented threat of a resumption of the nuclear arms race, to kill hope in the possibility of disarmament is, in a very real sense, to risk killing life itself.

---

*General Secretary Gorbachev has since gone even further in accepting on-site verification.

†This idea was later expanded to become the ten principles of "common ground." See Chapter 5, pp. 103–4.

DOCUMENT

DECLARATION ON SECURITY MADE BY THE COUNTRIES PARTICIPATING IN THE WILLIAMSBURG SUMMIT

WILLIAMSBURG, VIRGINIA, MAY 29, 1983

1. As leaders of our seven countries, it is our first duty to defend the freedom and justice on which our democracies are based. To this end, we shall maintain sufficient military strength to deter any attack, to counter any threat, and to ensure the peace. Our arms will never be used except in response to aggression.
2. We wish to achieve lower levels of arms through serious arms control negotiations. With this statement, we reaffirm our dedication to the search for peace and meaningful arms reductions. We are ready to work with the Soviet Union to this purpose and call upon the Soviet Union to work with us.
3. Effective arms control agreements must be based on the principle of equality and must be verifiable. Proposals have been put forward from the Western side to achieve positive results in various international negotiations: on strategic weapons (START), on intermediate-range nuclear missiles (INF), on chemical weapons, on reduction of forces in Central Europe (MBFR), and a Conference on Disarmament in Europe (CDE).
4. We believe that we must continue to pursue these negotiations with impetus and urgency. In the area of INF, in particular, we call upon the Soviet Union to contribute constructively to the success of the negotiations. Attempts to divide the West by proposing inclusion of the deterrent forces of third countries, such as those of France and the United Kingdom, will fail. Consideration of these systems has no place in the INF negotiations.
5. Our nations express the strong wish that a balanced INF agreement be reached shortly. Should this occur, the negotiations will determine the level of deployment. It is well known that should this not occur, the countries concerned will proceed with the planned deployment of the U.S. systems in Europe at the end of 1983.
6. Our nations are united in efforts for arms reductions and will continue to carry out thorough and intensive consultations. The security of our countries is indivisible and must be approached on a global basis. Attempts to avoid serious negotiation by seeking to influence public opinion in our countries will fail.
7. We commit ourselves to devote our full political resources to reducing the threat of war. We have a vision of a world in which the shadow of war has been lifted from all mankind, and we are determined to pursue that vision.*

---

*This is the first public use of the metaphor "lifting the shadow of war."

AN OPEN LETTER TO ALL CANADIANS

OTTAWA, MAY 9, 1983

In recent months I have received a great number of letters and petitions protesting against the possible testing of Cruise missiles in Canadian territory. . . .

Because this whole question continues to weigh heavily upon the consciences of those in government and the general public, I have now decided to address myself directly to Canadians through this open letter. My purpose is to explain the position of the Government of Canada on the testing of the Cruise missile, and on the broader issue of disarmament.

By way of a preamble, let me point out that our freedom to discuss and argue issues is what gives to our democracy its greatness and its strength; but that same freedom can also make us appear vulnerable in the face of Soviet totalitarianism.

In recent years, the Soviet Union has deployed hundreds of new SS-20 missiles, each equipped with three nuclear warheads, capable of reaching all the great cities of western Europe. However, there has not been any significant outburst of public opposition, either inside or outside the U.S.S.R.

That the Soviet people have not protested against this action of their leaders surprises no one. What is surprising, however, is that those in the West who are opposed to new nuclear weapons have remained relatively silent about the installation of the SS-20s. In contrast, they are now taking to the streets to oppose the possible deployment of American Pershing II and Cruise missiles to protect Europe against the Soviet nuclear threat.

What is particularly surprising in Canada is to see protesters opposing the possible testing of Cruise missiles in Canadian territory, but not opposing the fact that similar missiles are already being tested in the Soviet Union, as was confirmed in December by General-Secretary Andropov.

Because people in the free world feel powerless to influence the leaders of the U.S.S.R., there is a great temptation to direct the whole force of their anguish and their protests against the only decision-makers who are sensitive to public opinion, namely the leaders of the democratic countries. Having convinced themselves that it is useless to denounce the SS-20s, people find it easier, I suppose, to forget about them. The strange result of this forgetfulness is that it somehow becomes possible to portray the Soviet Union not as the aggressor, but as the innocent target. This represents a curious amnesia and reversal of roles, which the Soviet leaders are quick to exploit for their own purposes.

They hope, obviously, that one-sided information, and one-sided protests, will lead to the unilateral disarmament of the West. Indeed, there is a segment of public opinion in Western Europe which has already adopted that policy.

During the first special session on disarmament at the United Nations, I proposed, in the name of Canada, a strategy of suffocation. It was designed to smother, even in the laboratory, the development of any new nuclear weapons systems. Obviously, my proposal had to apply to both sides or to neither. There certainly was no suggestion in that proposal that the West should disarm unilaterally.

Because our strategy of suffocation was rejected by the Soviet Union, as evidenced by the continued deployment of the SS-20s, a weapon much superior to the SS-4 and 5, there was no question of urging its acceptance by the NATO countries alone. That is why we allied ourselves with the two-track strategy of our NATO partners. Those two tracks are to seek to negotiate the removal of the Soviet SS-20s, and at the same time, to prepare for the deployment of new American missiles in Europe so as to pressure the Soviet Union toward serious negotiations, and so as not to leave our European allies in a vulnerable position, if the negotiations on intermediate-range nuclear forces ended in failure.

Having declared our support for the two-track strategy, Canada should bear its fair share of the burden which that policy imposes upon the NATO alliance.

It is hardly fair to rely on the Americans to protect the West, but to refuse to lend them a hand when the going gets rough. In that sense, the anti-Americanism of some Canadians verges on hypocrisy. They're eager to take refuge under the American umbrella, but don't want to help hold it.

When we seek to apply moral principles to this issue, it's easy to become trapped in positions which are either too complex or too simple. The former can paralyze us. The latter can deceive us.

Into the trap of overcomplication fall those who insist that no moral position is valid which does not take into account every possible future breakthrough in nuclear weapons technology, every possible future difficulty in detecting the actions of the other side. Into a trap of oversimplification fall those who are content to talk about how many bowls of rice could be purchased for the price of a missile, or who condemn governments for spending anything at all on defence.

I do not deny that there is an element of truth and validity in an unconditionally pacifist position. I simply say that it is simplistic to ignore the real, complex, and often immoral world to which our moral choices must apply. The Pope himself recognized this fact in a message he sent last June to the second United Nations Special Session on Disarmament. ''In current conditions,'' he wrote, ''deterrence based on balance, certainly not as an end in itself, but as a step toward a progressive disarmament, may still be judged morally acceptable.''

I believe that the Soviet peoples desire peace just as much as the peoples of the free world. But I also know that the Soviets are very heavily armed. In these circumstances, it would be almost suicidal for the West to adopt a policy of unilateral disarmament, or a policy of suffocating the development of new means of defending ourselves against the Soviet SS-20s. That is the kind of heroic moral choice which an individual could make in his personal life, but does anyone have the right to impose that choice upon a whole nation, or upon the community of free countries?

When the choice is between steadfastness or weakness in the face of totalitarianism, history should have taught us that to refuse to risk one's life in defence of liberty is to risk losing liberty, without any guarantee of saving one's life.

That is why the Government of Canada has chosen, not without anguish or full awareness of the risk, to join our NATO partners in adopting a policy of strength in reaction to the Soviet Union.

In supporting the two-track strategy of the Atlantic alliance, however, we shall insist that progress be made simultaneously on both tracks. This combination of steadfastness of purpose and willingness to negotiate seems to be bearing fruit, as witness the latest offer of General-Secretary Andropov to take into account the numbers of warheads as well as missiles.

Indeed, are we to think that this new-found flexibility of Mr. Andropov is a straightforward show of goodwill? Are we to believe seriously that, on two occasions since last December, the Soviets would have contemplated publicly a reduction of their nuclear forces if we had weakened in our resolve?

To me, the answer is clear. And it is absolutely essential that the United States continue their efforts to negotiate the removal of the SS-20s in exchange for the non-deployment of new American missiles in Europe, or at least to negotiate smaller numbers of missiles on each side.

I hope that my explanation of our policy will have established that, were we to agree to collaborate in testing the guidance system of the Cruise missile, it would be because of our solidarity with the other Western democracies, in a world which has turned a deaf ear to our suggested strategy of suffocation.

That being said, however, I would add that we should not abandon hope for the ending of the nuclear arms race.

All the people of the world, whether they be friends or enemies, value their own lives, and the lives of those they love. If the discovery of the terrible secrets of the atom gives us the power to destroy the whole planet, there is a still more powerful force which can save it — our love for our children, and our love of life.

Therefore, I shall continue to believe that our strategy of suffocation is the best strategy.

The great powers of the world refuse to accept it now. But that will not stop us from repeating our proposal at every opportunity, until the recognition of its truth frees us all from moral anguish and from fear.

TRANSCRIPT OF THE PRIME MINISTER'S INTERVIEW WITH JACK CAHILL OF THE *TORONTO STAR*

TORONTO, MAY 14, 1983

Q. The testing of the Cruise has concerned a lot of people. Are you surprised at the numbers of people who protested that?

A. Not really. I think it is a very important cause. I have been, in my day, in nuclear protests, too. I have written on it in *Cité Libre** and I have been preoccupied with nuclear escalation and the possibility of nuclear war throughout my career, before being a prime minister and since being a prime minister.

As you know, I have denuclearized Canada in NATO; I have taken away our nuclear role in Europe. With the F-18s I am taking away any need for nuclear weapons to be stationed in Canada. I think I have done more in denuclearizing Canada than people realize.

Q. Yet, you are criticizing some of the protesters by saying that anti-American feelings over the possibility of the testing verges on hypocrisy; that, in effect, we live under the protection of the U.S. nuclear umbrella and that we have to lend a hand when asked. Is that not what you have been saying?

A. Well, quote me exactly if you are going to quote me in the article. I say "some Canadians who protest against the United States verge on hypocrisy," or words to that effect. It is obvious that in the thousands, and hundreds of thousands, maybe, of Canadians who are concerned about nuclear weapons, some are anti-American for the wrong reason. Some of them would very much like to wash their hands of the whole situation and say "Well of course, we rely on the nuclear umbrella, we rely on U.S. deterrence, but then let them fight their own battles and let us attack them when they propose to assist Europe with Euro-missiles."

... I think where there is confusion amongst a lot of the protesters is that they say that there are enough nuclear arms to destroy the enemy many times over and even to destroy most of humanity; that is a concern that I share and that is a fear that I have and that is the reason why I think there must be a limitation to nuclear arms.

But the argument on the Cruise is something else again. The Euromissiles are not something that the United States needs, they are something that the Europeans have asked for.

If those who protest against the Cruise have an argument, they should be protesting against the Europeans who have asked for Cruises and for Pershing IIs and who have said they want them deployed on their soil.

But when we protest against the Americans in this particular matter, some of it is ignorance and some of it is hypocrisy; some of it is sincere and some of it is enlightened, but I see nothing wrong in making that point.

---

* This was a reformist magazine published in Quebec during the 1950s. Mr. Trudeau was an editor of it.

The reason that Canada has accepted an umbrella agreement with the United States — which might or might not lead to Cruise testing — is largely because of NATO policy. And it is once again not the Americans who have convinced us that the two-track policy is right; it was asked, first, by Chancellor Schmidt, who was the head of the Socialist Government in Germany; it was asked by our other allies in Europe — the French, the British, the Italians.

Mr. Trudeau created a "new look" foreign policy for Canada, but paid tribute to his predecessor, Lester B. ("Mike") Pearson, in doing so. Many foreign policy analysts have noted the similarities between the fundamental approaches of the two leaders. However, Mr. Trudeau sought to reorganize the foreign policy-making machinery of government inherited from the 1950s and 1960s and largely succeeded in doing so.

Mr. Trudeau was the first foreign leader to meet with newly elected President Richard Nixon (March 24, 1969). Although the two men had very different personalities, Mr. Trudeau had a professional, businesslike approach to meetings with Mr. Nixon. The two agreed to end all rhetoric of a "special relationship" between Canada and the United States in favour of pragmatic efforts to resolve conflicts.

When Mr. Trudeau took office, controversy over the war in Vietnam was reaching a peak. As illustrated by this photograph taken on August 9, 1969 in Vancouver, British Columbia, he had no fear of dissent and readily waded into demonstrations to debate with his opponents.

The photograph at top of page 61 is from Robert Cooper. All remaining photographs are from Canapress Photo Service.

Mr. Trudeau established personal early contacts with the leaders of the Soviet Union. Here, he ushered then Soviet Foreign Minister Andrei Gromyko into the garden at the Prime Minister's official residence, 24 Sussex Drive, Ottawa (October 3, 1969). In the spring of 1971, Mr. Trudeau made the first visit by a Canadian Prime Minister to the Soviet Union.

An early priority for Mr. Trudeau was recognition of the People's Republic of China. In 1973, he cemented new ties by visiting the country which had captured his imagination during a personal visit in 1960. He shared a state banquet with Premier Chou En-lai, October 11, 1973.

During his China visits, Mr. Trudeau examined the caves of Kweilin with then Vice-Premier Deng Zhao Ping, now the main leader in China (October 1973).

An early visit abroad to India allowed Mr. Trudeau to form a long-standing political relationship with Prime Minister Indira Gandhi (January 11, 1971).

Jauntily wearing a rose in his lapel — his trademark — Mr. Trudeau greeted U.S. Secretary of State Henry Kissinger on June 18, 1974 during a two-day NATO summit meeting held in Ottawa. Mr. Trudeau constantly pressed for more debates in NATO councils and fewer set-piece speeches. He pressed for NATO to become a political as well as a military body, capable of taking collective initiatives for arms control as well as for arms modernization.

Pierre Trudeau had high hopes that in President Jimmy Carter he had found an American leader with similar views. But instead, the Canadian-American relationship grew more difficult. The two men stood together as anthems played for the Trudeau visit to Washington, February 21, 1977, just after President Carter took office.

In July 1975, Mr. Trudeau took part in the Helsinki Summit, and conferred with Soviet Leader Leonid Brezhnev on July 31. Throughout his time in office, Mr. Trudeau stressed the theme of human rights with the Soviets.

Mr. Trudeau had a warm friendship with West German Chancellor Helmut Schmidt. They met at Vancouver International Airport, July 7, 1977.

President Gerald Ford and Mr. Trudeau had a cordial relationship. Here they skied together in Vail, Colorado, after Mr. Ford had left office (December 30, 1977).

Relations between the developed countries and the Third World were a frequent concern to Mr. Trudeau and led to his efforts to promote a "North-South dialogue." In early 1981 he visited countries in Europe, Africa, and Latin America to seek support for a North-South Summit later that year. In this photo, five Nigerian boys wait under a tree for Mr. Trudeau to pass through the town of Maiduguri on January 11, 1981.

Mr. Trudeau enjoyed his contacts with President Julius Nyerere of Tanzania. They met August 18, 1981 at the State House in Dar Es Galaum, in preparation for the North-South Summit to take place in October of that year.

Canada's relations with France improved considerably with the election of François Mitterand as President. The two men met on April 19, 1982, when Mr. Mitterand landed in Vancouver on his way back from Japan.

After many summit meetings, Mr. Trudeau longed for greater informality and fewer precooked releases. He showed this frustration after the Bonn Summit, June 10, 1982, by facetiously redirecting reporters' questions from Ronald Reagan to Secretary of State Alexander Haig. Others in the picture included from left: Italian Foreign Minister Columbo, NATO Secretary-General Lunns, West German Foreign Minister Gevscher, and Prime Minister Thatcher.

During the Trudeau years, there were regular contacts on bilateral problems with senior U.S. officials. U.S. Secretary of State George Shultz was relaxed in Mr. Trudeau's company at a luncheon held for him in Ottawa, October 25, 1982.

As one of his first acts in office, Mr. Trudeau reduced the Canadian armed forces, believing social programme expenditures to be more important than what he thought were overextended military commitments abroad. Between 1969 and 1984, Canada became the first nuclear power ever to give up nuclear weapons. Nevertheless, Mr. Trudeau also presided over a substantial modernization of armed forces equipment and training. Here, he visits the Canadian base in Lahr, West Germany, and drives a Leopard tank under the direction of Lieutenant Jon MacIntyre (November 11, 1982).

Canada maintained a strong commitment to the Middle East peace process during the Trudeau years. In January 1983, Egyptian President Hosni Mubarak met with Mr. Trudeau in Ottawa. Behind them is the Gothic "West Block" of the Canadian Parliament Buildings.

Following his "peace initiative" meeting with President Reagan, Mr. Trudeau and the President addressed the press in the Rose Garden, December 15, 1983. Mr. Trudeau and the President stressed the importance of communicating the desire to negotiate with the Soviet Union as well as to be strong militarily. Those looking on rather glumly include from left to right: Richard Burt, the senior U.S. State Department official responsible for Canada; Robert MacFarlane, former National Security Council head; U.S. Ambassador to Canada Paul Robinson; Defence Secretary Caspar Weinberger; and Secretary of State George Shultz, from left to right. Mr. Trudeau subsequently called those U.S. officials who derided his initiative "pipsqueaks from the Pentagon."

On January 16, 1984, Mr. Trudeau met with the leaders of several Canadian peace and labour groups, including Canadian Labour Congress President Dennis McDermott. McDermott was a bitter opponent of the Trudeau government on every other subject but arms control. (He was appointed Ambassador to Ireland by the Mulroney government.) From left to right of Mr. McDermott are Canadian Labour Congress Director of International Relations John Harker, Brigadier General Maurice Archdeacon, defence policy advisor to Mr. Trudeau, and Dr. Paul Cappon, Physicians for Social Responsibility. Behind Mr. Trudeau is Jim Stark, head of Operation Dismantle.

During the Davos Symposium in Switzerland, Mr. Trudeau and Raymond Barre, former Prime Minister of France, had a heated debate about whether the United States would be the first to use nuclear weapons if attacked by conventional Warsaw Pact forces (January 29, 1984).

Mr. Trudeau maintained friendships with several European leaders, including Swedish European Prime Minister Olof Palme to whom this book is dedicated. The two men met in New York while Palme was Ambassador to the United Nations, prior to his return to Sweden (September 30, 1983).

After giving a lengthy speech in which he summed up his peace initiative and set out ten points of "common ground" between East and West, Mr. Trudeau sat pensively in his seat in the House of Commons. Fellow Liberal MP's applauded around him. Beside him was Deputy Prime Minister and Secretary of State for External Affairs Allan J. MacEachen. Under the Canadian system, the Prime Minister appears almost daily for opposition questioning during the hour-long "Question Period" (February 9, 1984).

On January 31, 1984, Mr. Trudeau visited East German leader Erich Honecker; he proposed that middlepowers such as Canada and East Germany develop their own initiatives to reduce tensions, operating within their respective alliances.

On November 13, 1984 Mr. Trudeau received the Einstein Peace Prize in Washington, D.C. Norman Cousins appeared with him in this photo.

Chapter 4

Developing the Peace Initiative

INTRODUCTION

O n September 1, 1983, a Korean airliner en route to Japan from Anchorage, Alaska, suddenly disappeared from radar screens. It had been shot down over the Sea of Japan after entering Soviet air space. Flight 007 was carrying 269 passengers and crew, including ten Canadians: all were lost.

The Canadian responses — condemnation, suspension of Soviet airline landing rights in Canada, and the demand for compensation — paralleled those of other Western nations. But there was a "second track" of reaction as well.

Prime Minister Trudeau was deeply concerned about the lack of security and other underlying causes of the disaster. Despite Opposition arguments in the House of Commons, he refused to express unrelenting outrage against the Soviet Union, arguing that "I can express indignation as well as the Leader of the Opposition . . . [but] there should be some effort to re-establish communications with the Soviets." He argued that the superpowers "must find some way to stop shouting at each other, when the world is teetering on the brink of disaster and atomic war."

At about the same time as this defence was being mounted in the House of Commons, a team of senior officials and experts was hurriedly assembled from various federal agencies, including the Prime Minister's Office, the Department of External Affairs, and the Department of National Defence. They pulled together a package of proposals to use as a "calling card" for the Prime Minister to take to the nations directly and indirectly involved in the escalation of tension.

Mr. Trudeau gave the first hints of this package in a toast to British Prime Minister Margaret Thatcher when she visited Toronto on September 26, 1983 (pp. 65–66).

After working their way through twenty-six different arms control proposals of greater or lesser feasibility, officials suggested a few that might be especially useful to the Prime Minister. He quashed the reservations they had about the whole enterprise. It was clear that there would be cynicism about his plans among the Canadian electorate; they now regarded virtually every government initiative as a last-ditch attempt to remain in office.*

In a speech to an international conference of noted arms control experts and interested persons held in Guelph, Ontario, Mr. Trudeau set out his overall approach, calling for political decision-makers to take over from the "nuclear accountants" who had appropriated arms control talks (pp. 67–74). He next embarked on a round of meetings with European leaders including those of Great Britain, France, Belgium, The Netherlands, Italy, the Vatican, and West Germany, seeking their support. The proposals which he had taken to them and their reactions were reported in detail to a meeting in Montreal on November 13 (pp. 75–80). In Mr. Trudeau's retrospective view the most interesting meeting was with Prime Minister Margaret Thatcher. Although the two leaders had met a few weeks previously, there was an apparent British desire for another round. European leaders *wanted* to be seen to be discussing the Canadian peace initiative.

A final document which belongs as part of the "peace initiative" proposals is the Speech from the Throne opening a new session of the Canadian Parliament on December 7, 1983. This document is prepared under the direction of the Prime Minister for the Governor-General to read. It is a comprehensive statement of policy and legislative intentions similar to the State of the Union Address in the United States. In this case, the "peace initiative" was made a central element of the Government's program for 1984 (p. 81).

---

*The opinion polls showed the Liberals trailing the opposition Progressive Conservatives. Speculation about Mr. Trudeau's own retirement was rife.

TRANSCRIPT OF A TOAST BY PRIME MINISTER TRUDEAU TO PRIME MINISTER MARGARET THATCHER, AT A DINNER IN HER HONOUR

TORONTO, SEPTEMBER 26, 1983

We live in a world of change, a world where questions have replaced certitudes. Today you and I have discussed some of the critical questions of our times — political, economic, and security questions which trouble the people of our two countries. We discussed them openly and candidly, as only friends can....

Canada has developed and grown strong because of the vitality of its democracy, and because of the skills and values brought here from Britain, France, and many other countries.

Nowhere is our partnership more vital than in the pursuit of peace. Canada and the United Kingdom are committed members of NATO. For our part...we Canadians look upon NATO as the cornerstone of our defence policy.

We do not wish to be silent partners, however. It is a political alliance, after all, and politicians like to discuss and even argue the issues. If we disagree from time to time, and expend great effort in trying to resolve our differences, that is not a sign of weakness in the Alliance, but a sign of the strength which pervades a free association of independent countries.

Because all of us live under the threat of the mushroom cloud, I believe it is incumbent upon all nations — whether they be neutral, non-aligned, or members of alliances — to apply every effort to bring about an arms reduction agreement between the superpowers.

It is true, of course, that Canada, like other nations, does not sit at the negotiating table with the United States and the Soviet Union. But that does not mean that our interests and our lives are not on the table. We depend upon the wisdom of the leadership of our alliance, but that does not mean that we can do nothing ourselves.

I do not underestimate the difficulty of achieving a disarmament agreement between East and West. On the contrary, I believe the task becomes more difficult every day, and that fact alone gives added urgency to our effort.

One of the reasons why success at the negotiating table has proven so difficult is that strategic issues have become almost infinitely complex. The temptation is strong for leaders of non-superpowers to leave the technicalities to their experts, and the strategies themselves to the United States and to the Soviet Union. There is also a political temptation to adopt the seductive thought that, since we are not at the table, we cannot be blamed for failure there.

But such is the growing magnitude of the threat against us all that we can no longer justify yielding the most important issue of our lives to the nuclear accountants and technical experts. We must get involved.

We must avoid the trap of allowing the debate to be conducted on purely technical grounds, where the weapons technicians can use their expert knowledge to consign everyone else to the fringes of relevancy. The experts do not have the responsibility for the fate of the earth. Political leaders, however, do.

So we must look to politics, rather than technology, to find ways to ensure that the fateful button is not pushed without full understanding of the actions or intentions of the other side.

Let us work together to establish better communication and understanding between the Eastern and Western alliances, so as to reduce the possibility that decisions may be made through ignorance or miscalculation of each other's attitudes.

As Lord Carrington said a few months ago, we cannot go on facing down the Russians in a silent war of nerves, punctuated by periods of megaphone diplomacy.

There is no issue more important than the control, the limiting, and the reduction of armaments. There is no higher priority for leaders than to work together toward those goals.

In that spirit . . . I hope it will be possible for us to have further consultations in the future.

The forthcoming Conference on Disarmament in Europe will afford an opportunity to achieve real movement toward our goal.*

Such steps may seem small at first, but they can begin to build the confidence that is needed between East and West.

Confidence, however, is fragile. It is based, on our side at least, on one of our keystone values — the willing acceptance of responsibility for one's actions.

In that context, the shooting down of an unarmed, civilian airplane is a shocking reminder that we live in a world which is dangerously close to disaster, where a single horrendous deed has the potential of setting off a cataclysm. For that reason alone, it is vital the NATO demonstrate solidarity, credibility, and wisdom . . . .

---

* Mr. Trudeau noted in comments to the editor of this book that people in Western Europe were rightfully sceptical about yet another initiative in the European arms control field. In particular, talks on mutual and balanced conventional force reductions had created a climate of cynicism. This climate is what led Canada to propose that the Stockholm effort on "confidence-building measures" start at the highest *political* level possible and why this was so important. In September 1986, the Stockholm Conference *did* produce an agreement on confidence-building measures, especially on troop movements and military exercises in Europe.

REFLECTIONS ON PEACE AND SECURITY*

GUELPH, ONTARIO, OCTOBER 27, 1983

...The name of Guelph reminds us of another age which was torn by hostile systems, competing alliances, and profound ideological division. The depth and violence of the dispute between Guelphs and Ghibellines tore Europe apart for much of the twelfth and thirteenth centuries. The argument was fundamental for the time. Who was supreme, Pope or Emperor? It spread from Germany to Italy, France, and Sicily, drawing other powers and interests in its wake. No country, church, class, or family in Europe was immune from the destructive force of that question.

Popes excommunicated emperors. Emperors took up arms against successive popes. The battle between Guelphs and Ghibellines was remarkable for its ferocity, for the loss of life and the wreck of cities, for its pervasive and lasting influence throughout European politics and culture. It was an early version of total war — on a continental scale. And, because both history and geography are written by the victorious, the name of Guelph lives on, given to this place as the proud heritage of a ruling dynasty.

That this city... is to be found in Canada encourages me to underline a further proposition, familiar but profound: that we Canadians have a framework of long-standing and deep-rooted ties with European conflicts. There is a European-ness, well beyond place-names, in our history, in our culture, and in the predisposition of many government policies. I do no disservice to our North American nature nor to our place on the Pacific Rim. But our engagement with Europe comes home with particular force in questions of peace and security.

Canada's participation, from the beginning, in both World Wars of this century, our founding and loyal membership in NATO, our decision to test the Cruise missile in Canadian territory, all demonstrate the recognition that our own security is tightly bound with the security of our European allies.

A nation of our size and geographic location could, in the past or in the present, have considered other options. These options, whether of isolationism, or of being a nuclear-weapons state ourselves, have in Canada been invariably set aside in favour of a commitment to collective security. Our dedication to the Western alliance, and to our partnership with the United States in the defence of this continent, is part of the bedrock of our foreign policy.

But the political, economic, and military obligations we have undertaken for our common defence offer commensurate rights and duties. Among them is the right to speak about the full range of Western policies, and the duty to reflect about where we are and where we should be going.

We are not silent partners in any of the councils we have joined — because silence would mean the abdication of responsibility in the face of crisis. We are not ambiguous about our international commitments — because we recognize our deep engagement with an interdependent world. We are not afraid to negotiate with those who may threaten us — because that fear would betray lack of confidence in the vital strength of our own values.

---

*Parts of this speech originally delivered in French; here translated into English.

That is...the spirit in which I want to share some of my own reflections on the theme of "Strategies for Peace and Security in the Nuclear Age."

I will tell you right away that I am deeply troubled: by an intellectual climate of acrimony and uncertainty; by the parlous state of East-West relations; by a superpower relationship which is dangerously confrontational; and by a widening gap between military strategy and political purpose. All these reveal most profoundly the urgent need to assert the pre-eminence of the mind of man over machines of war.

There is today an ominous rhythm of crisis. Not just an arms crisis. It is a crisis of confidence in ourselves, a crisis of faith in others. How can we change that ominous rhythm?...

I start from...the difficulty all of us experience in trying to know what is going on in the world — to know it and to understand it in a manner that is accurate, that provides the ground for useful actions.

Too often our knowledge and our judgements are true and false at the same time. This is often the distinctive sign of rapidly changing realities which tend to elude our understanding. For example, we know that there are, in the eighties, many new kinds of power and many new centres of power. There is the power of oil, or of cheap labour, or of regional hegemony. We call it a multipolar world — which suggests that no nation can act in isolation, that no power is truly dominant. But surely it is also true, and perhaps now with a special force, that the superpower relationship is at this time as dominant and as critical as it ever was in the fifties — when we had a more simplistic bipolar model with which to understand the world.

Another example: military strategy is the subject of much debate these days. This is a positive sign. Many strategists, in rightly trying to increase the odds against the nuclear gamble, advocate increased strength in conventional weapons, and new doctrines for conventional deterrence. Some of these doctrines have the sound purpose of delaying, or even preventing, the terrible resort to nuclear weapons in any European conflict.

I believe that such a raising of the nuclear threshold in Europe is a concept of the first importance. It would not be an easy, or an inexpensive task. But even as I am attracted to this concept in its application to Europe, I am troubled by a broader implication. Non-nuclear weapons are in an advanced state of technology, and are widely marketed. Sea-skimming missiles, laser-guided bombs, and fragmentation weapons are available for distribution. Is it the purpose of nuclear arms controls to make the world safe for conventional warfare of an increasingly terrifying nature?

Surely a basic term is missing in this equation: it is the encouragement of an equilibrium of conventional arms and forces, balanced at *lower* rather than higher levels. An agreed framework of conventional deterrence against armed aggression — but significantly reducing any dangerous concentration of forces.

This is to some extent the task of the Mutual and Balanced Force Reduction Talks in Vienna. But those talks will not succeed unless their importance in terms of military strategy is developed within a wider framework of East-West confidence and political will.

Let me suggest yet a further example of our difficulty in understanding a time which appears to be out of joint. A moment ago I used the word interdependence. It is the accepted description of the world as we know it. I think it described a rational and positive condition, an ethic to be encouraged. But we are also learning that the consequences of interdependence are frequently unforeseen, often irrational, negative, and out of control — rogue trends which promote inequality among states, and deep strains between them.

When I was first thinking about and writing this speech, I was tempted to give the example of Poland. But now, obviously, the example of this is Grenada, which shows that if you are an interdependent world, you cannot be equally interdependent with two major powers. And if you try to be friendly with both, it does not work out.

If we have difficulty understanding the intricacies of interdependence, we are not yet even close to managing the economic linkages with peace and security.

Consider Poland. Its economic collapse strongly suggested action to assist. Western banks were deeply exposed. There seemed to be a common interest in the renewed viability of the Polish economy. But the overriding political considerations, in light of the brutal declaration of martial law, pointed in quite the opposite direction.

Thus, the debate over East-West economic relations — which haunts every Western council — reveals the fundamental and unresolved question of how much economic interdependence is desirable between the two systems. Some say less. Some say more. Those who argue for less are often, paradoxically, the first to advocate the punitive merit of economic sanctions — which are only effective, after all, if interdependence exists, and if Soviet behaviour is modified by the expectation of economic benefit. Moreover, some who argue for economic sanctions in the civilian sector apparently believe that this will influence Soviet military spending. Yet they may add that there is little, if any, relationship between civilian and military economies in the Soviet Union.

This particular debate . . . tends also to lay open one of the most gaping self-inflicted wounds of the current period. That is the unfortunate tendency for a discussion which starts off about East-West relations to wind up in the fratricide of West-West relations. There have been days when I, or Ronald Reagan, or Margaret Thatcher may seem to have been accused, for whatever reason or passion of the moment, of posing a greater threat to the security of the West than do the Russians and their associates.

It is almost as though the diversity, pluralism, and freedom of expression which we are determined to preserve *through* the Alliance, are not seen as appropriate *within* the Alliance.

The alliance in arms against itself is a paradox rich with historical allusion. NATO will avoid that fate if we are wise. But institutions cannot grow to meet new challenges if their level of debate — their intellectual universe of discourse — does not expand to meet the changing realities of our environment.

Therefore, I am uneasy with these paradoxes. I am not satisfied with our ability to analyze and understand the complexities of an entirely new phase in East-West relations. I am not reassured by the posture and rhetoric of an earlier wartime age — an age, by the way, in which Canadian nerves were not found to falter.

For it is not our nerves which are being tested now, and these are not the playing fields on which we stand and cheer. These are the killing-grounds of life itself — and what is being tested is whether the force and will of our statecraft can reverse the momentum of the nuclear arms race . . . .

How did we arrive at such an impasse? Some of the answers lie in the ragged course of East-West relations over the past 15 years. Those relations have an innate tendency to defy management and control. They are animated by competing philosophies and civilizations, and armed with weaponry that is global in scope. [T]he two sides advocate radically different visions of political order, human values, and social behaviour.

As Canadians, we know where we stand. We have a distinguished record of accomplishment in working for international peace and security. NATO has, without doubt, been one of the instruments preventing nuclear war for the past 35 years. Canada has done pioneering work in the United Nations and elsewhere on arms control and disarmament.... Our nuclear power industry has perforce made us experts on safeguards agreements and has given us a special commitment to the cause of non-proliferation. We have continuously pressed for a comprehensive nuclear test ban treaty, for a convention to prohibit chemical weapons, and for the prohibition of all weapons for use in outer space.

...We have identified a distinctive Canadian space in East-West relations, determined by our history and geography, by our membership in NATO, by successive waves of immigration, by such priorities as trade and human rights, and by that sense of realism which is... both the achievement and the comfort of the middlepower's middle age.

I don't believe we had any illusions about the short-lived and much-maligned period of détente. I certainly have no embarrassment about my own part in that process, bred in a conjuncture of geopolitics, economic aspirations, and collective leadership on both sides.

But the process too soon became part of the problem. The main achievements of the late sixties and early seventies were carried forward with difficulty, perhaps with an overload of linkage. Historians may reflect on the reasons why 1975 was the year which saw both the high point of the formal structure of détente in the conclusion of the Helsinki Final Act — and the imminent erosion of its broader purpose as a result, mainly, I think, of Soviet-Cuban adventurism in Angola.

Détente rapidly showed signs of a process being drained of its substance. Core issues were held hostage by one side or the other — human rights, economic co-operation, hegemony in key spheres of influence. Détente became both divisible, and reversible.

And yet, I am not ready to call détente a failure. There were clear benefits of stability and co-operation. Its long-term impact, for example on Soviet élites, cannot yet be judged. Moreover, it did coincide with, or provoke, an important impulse in the early seventies which seems to have been lost without trace. It is the impulse toward political dialogue, toward regular consultation at the most senior levels of the East-West system.

This was not talk for the sake of talk. It led to a set of interlocking bargains or understandings on strategic arms, on Vietnam, on the place of China in the world, on co-operation in outer space. And there are many other examples. Techniques of crisis management were put tenuously in place. It was an impulse in which elements of mutual respect contended with the search for advantage — which is to say it was high politics in action.

With the loss of that impulse, and in the absence of high politics in the East-West relationship, it is not surprising that any shred of trust or confidence in the intentions of the other side appears to have vanished as well. Also missing, and this troubles me greatly, is much trace of political craft and creativity directed at... *improving* the intentions of the other side. There is a disturbing complacency, a readiness to adapt to the worst rather than to exert our influence for the better. We are, in short, depoliticizing the most important political relationship we have.

The responsibility for this lies partly, but by no means exclusively, with both superpowers. The United States and the Soviet Union outstrip the rest of us in their global reach, their armaments, and their leadership responsibilities. Naturally, they differ greatly — and I am not committing the fallacy of describing them as equals in any moral sense at all. Nevertheless, they breathe an atmosphere common to themselves, and share a global perception according to which even remote events can threaten their interests or their associates.

And there are some other features which both powers have in common: continental land-mass and considerable economic self-sufficiency; ambivalent relationships with Europe and with Asia; complexities of demography; a central focus on each other in their policies; spasms of unilateralism or isolationism.

It is therefore all too facile to deny the grave responsibilities which are shared in Washington and Moscow, or to deny that what both seem to lack at the present time is a political vision of the world wherein both their nations can live in peace. What is essential to assert is that, just as war is too important to leave to the generals, so the relationship between the superpowers may have become too charged with animosity for East-West relations to be entrusted to them alone.

Military scientists make a routine distinction between capabilities — what weaponry the enemy has; and intentions — when, how, and why he intends to use it. I am profoundly concerned that we are devoting far too great a proportion of our time to the enumeration of capabilities, and far too little to the assessment of intentions which govern the use of arms. We may at some point be able to freeze the nuclear capability in the world at greatly reduced levels. But how do we freeze the menacing intentions... which remain? Therein lies the inadequacy of some of the nuclear freeze arguments.

Although known as the architect of total war, Von Clausewitz himself insisted on a political framework for military capabilities. He said that: "War cannot be separated from political life, whenever this occurs in our thinking... we have before us a senseless thing without an object."

On that point, I agree with him. I am convinced that casting a fresh linkage — of military strategy with, and subordinate to, strong political purpose — must become the highest priority of East and West alike.

This is a period of deep questioning of many of the strategic concepts which have dominated the post-war world. "New School" strategists, and critics from left and from right, are probing the fundamentals of strategic thought in the nuclear age from many points of view. They are in agreement, however, when they point to changing realities, to evolution in the psychology of those who live constantly with the spectre of nuclear war, and to the importance of weeding out obsolete ideas.

But much of this questioning, provocative as it is, strikes me as missing an important point. And that is the place of military strategy in the nuclear age. I believe that military strategy must, above all, serve a comprehensive set of political objectives and controls, which dominate and give purpose to modern weapons and military doctrine. Our central purpose must be to create a stable environment of increased security for both East and West. We must aim at suppressing those nearly instinctive fears, frustrations, or ambitions which have so often been the reason for resorting to the use of arms.

Therefore it is essential to Western purposes, in my judgement, to maintain in our policies elements of communication, negotiation, and transparency about our own intentions — plus a measure of incentive for the Soviet Union first to clarify, and then to modify, its own objectives toward the West.

This was, in a limited sense, the philosophy which underpinned the NATO response to the Soviet build-up of SS-20 missiles in Europe. We had to ask ourselves what purpose of political intimidation could be served by that build-up. That is why we decided to respond with a two-track approach — deployment and negotiations. This approach has given the Soviet Union both the clear incentive to reach agreement, and the table at which to do so. I and my fellow NATO heads of government remain firmly committed to that two-track decision.

The tragic shooting down of the Korean airliner raises further questions about military dominance on the Soviet side. Is the Soviet military system edging beyond the reach of the political authorities? Are we contributing to such a trend by the absence of regular contact with the Soviet leadership?

These considerations suggest that our two-track decision may also require, as the time for deployment comes closer, a "third rail" of high-level political energy to speed the course of agreement — a third rail through which might run the current of our broader political purposes, including our determination not to be intimidated.

The risk of accident or miscalculation is too great for us not to begin to repair the lines of communication with our adversaries. The level of tension is too high for us not to revive a more constructive approach to the containment of crises. The degree of mutual mistrust is too intense for us not to try to rebuild confidence through active political contact and consultation.

Only in this way can the quality and credibility of efforts toward peace and security, from whatever quarter, East or West, be animated and reinforced. But it is a precondition of that goal that Western councils, particularly at the head of government level, benefit from the free flow of ideas which we maintain in our own societies, and which we advocate for others. That, too, forms part of our armament and we should not hesitate to deploy it.

Because the trend is for arms negotiations, like military strategy itself, to become ever more distanced from the political energy of the participants. I have mentioned the [Mutual and Balanced Force Reduction] talks in Vienna. That forum has laboured for over ten years and produced very little by way of results. Those talks require urgent political attention if they are to move off dead centre. Over the years, other leaders and I have made several proposals in that direction — proposals which now merit wider support.

And by the way, ministerial attention does get action. I welcome the decision made...by NATO defence ministers...to withdraw, unilaterally, approximately 1,400 tactical nuclear warheads from stocks in Europe. You will recall a similar decision...in 1979...resulted in a withdrawal of 1,000. But just taking this 1,400, that is about one-quarter of the nuclear warheads that NATO has in Europe. So, some say that these moves are limited, but even limited steps in the right direction take on importance in dangerous times.

We have high hopes for the Conference on Disarmament in Europe...due to open in Stockholm next January. Canada will do its utmost to make that Conference productive. We recognize the importance of agreement on confidence-building measures of a military nature. But these negotiations, important as they are, will not advance our larger hopes if they proceed in a political vacuum. The delicate framework of security in Europe cannot be balanced on the fate of one or two sets of negotiations alone. These negotiations must be grounded in a structure of stable East-West understanding: reciprocal acknowledgement of legitimate security needs, regular high-level dialogue, and a determined approach to crisis management. Here, again, we require that jolt of political energy which I have described as the "third rail."

What is missing is a strategy of confidence-building measures of a *political* nature:

— steps that reduce tensions caused by uncertainty about objectives, or caused by fear of the consequences of failure;
— steps that mitigate hostility and promote a modicum of mutual respect;
— steps that build an authentic confidence in man's ability to survive on this planet.

In short, we must take positive political steps in order to reverse the dangerously downward trend-line in East-West relations, which has been sloping downward for much too long. . . .

The negotiations in the theatre of nuclear forces in Europe, and on strategic forces, are taking place between the superpowers. Canada is not at the table, and we have no wish to insert ourselves into this vital and delicate process. It is my hope, however, that we might help to influence the prospects of early agreement. We need to be realistic about the hard factors in play. We must appreciate the primordial drive for security and for sovereignty which is never very far below the surface of the arms control debate.

I intend to speak further, in other speeches in the weeks ahead, about these issues of confidence, stability, arms control, and political will, which dominate not only our times, but our lives as well. I have this week begun a process of close discussion with President Reagan. My consultations with other leaders have already commenced. I can announce tonight that, within the next two weeks, I shall be seeing President Mitterand in Paris, Prime Minister Lubbers in The Hague, Prime Minister Martens in Brussels, Prime Minister Craxi in Rome, and Chancellor Kohl in Bonn.* I plan to take to them in person my own recommendations for a strategy of political confidence-building.

We will want to look at several elements, some of which I can mention tonight:

— ways of designing a consistent structure of political and economic confidence with which to stabilize East-West relations;
— ways to draw the superpowers away from their concentration on military strength toward regular and productive dialogue, toward a sense of responsibility commensurate with their power;
— ways to persuade all five nuclear weapons states to engage in negotiations aimed at establishing global limits on their strategic nuclear arsenals;
— ways of improving European security through the raising of the nuclear threshold, including the imposition of a political dynamic upon the static MBFR talks in Vienna; and
— ways to arrest the horizontal proliferation of nuclear weapons among other states.

It is my personal purpose to live up to the undertaking, made by leaders at

---

* He also saw Margaret Thatcher of Great Britain at her request, even though they had already met on the subject in September.

the Williamsburg Summit last May, "to devote our full political resources to reducing the threat of war." The questions to be raised . . . are not easy. There are priorities which inevitably conflict. A new climate of East-West confidence cannot be instilled in a day, nor can the arms race be stopped overnight. But insofar as I, and other leaders who share this purpose, can work together to build authentic confidence, I pledge to you that we shall.

Not to do so at this time would, I believe, amount to a form of escapism — an escapism well defined by the Harvard Nuclear Study Group in their thoughtful book, *Living with Nuclear Weapons*. The book cautions against two forms of escapism: the first form is to believe that nuclear weapons will go away. The authors rightly and regretfully say that they will not. But the second form of escapism, they point out, is to think that nuclear weapons can be treated like any other military weapons in history. Surely it is clear that they cannot.

And therefore I would add a third form of escapism, which we indulge in at our peril. That is the escapism of allowing shrill rhetoric to become a substitute for foreign policy, of letting inertia become a substitute for will, of making a desert and calling it peace . . . .

REMARKS BY THE PRIME MINISTER ON PEACE AND SECURITY*

MONTREAL, NOVEMBER 13, 1983

. . . If our future depended on Canadians alone, we could be confident that it was safe and sound. But no nation today holds its future securely in its own hands. We share this planet with about 160 other nations, all of whom interact with us in a global system embracing our security, our economy, the health of our environment, and the quality of our lives.

Those 160 governments are, however, by no means the only players. The stage is crowded with alliances, with regional associations, with international institutions such as the United Nations, with multinational corporations, with cartels, pressure groups, and lobbies of all kinds.

We are all of us — you and I, our friends and families, citizens, governments, and corporations — on that crowded global stage, which is alive with our hopes and our fears, our failures and our successes. But there are today three dominant and disturbing trends which, when set side by side, threaten to bring down the curtain on our human performance.

The first trend is an increasing resort to the use of force in the settlement of international disputes. Despite the solemn affirmation of the UN Charter that "all members shall refrain in their international relations from the threat or use of force," there have been, since 1945, approximately 130 conflicts in which 35 million human lives have been lost.

There is a habit of aggression which is gaining ground. An abdication of the political process in deference to military solutions. A coarse element of belligerence, of menacing rhetoric, of governments which rise and fall at gunpoint. The trend is global — and it is gathering speed.

This brutalization of political life takes on a particularly dangerous tone when it is driven by the clash of confrontational ideologies, and armed with sophisticated weapons. Weapons claiming an annual expenditure on the order of 600 billion dollars for nuclear and conventional arms combined. Weapons claiming too great a share of the budgets of impoverished Third World nations. Weapons which promote a rising tide of violence and engulf more peaceful ways to resolve disputes. That is the first trend: the brutalization of international relations.

The second trend is the steady unravelling of the international régime designed to prevent the proliferation of nuclear weapons.

We are today preoccupied mainly with the evident need to assert restraint over the arsenals of all five nuclear powers. But from a global perspective, and in the near term, the consequences of horizontal proliferation to other states pose an equally grave threat. Perhaps more grave, since the use of nuclear weapons by other nations would be unchecked by the assurance of mutual destruction which obtains among the five powers.

It was precisely to arrest both kinds of proliferation that a formal agreement

---

*This speech has been slightly edited by Mr. Trudeau to improve its clarity. Major portions of the speech were given in French and appear here in translation.

— the Non-Proliferation Treaty — came into effect in 1970, and is up for review in 1985....

The treaty stands now at a crossroads between peaceful aspiration and military strategy. It is the crossroads at which nuclear and non-nuclear countries — East and West, North and South — preoccupied with their survival, with their sovereignty, or with current conflicts, will decide whether the covenant still holds.

The third trend which threatens the global system is the worsening state of relations between East and West, particularly of relations between the two superpowers....

I ask you now to consider these three trends in relation to each other — laminated together, as they are in real life. An increasing resort to the use of force. The growing reality of the proliferation of nuclear weapons. And a superpower relationship charged with animosity. I believe it is evident that only a global approach to peace and security can reverse the path of this sinister, composite trend-line.

Because, as tensions build, the East-West relationship becomes particularly vulnerable to events on the periphery. An endemic instability is evident in areas largely understood to be the sphere of influence of one or the other superpower. At other flash points, such as the ever volatile Middle East, we see the tinder for a spreading conflagration.

The penetration of East-West rivalry into the Third World will reach its deepest and most dangerous point if, despite the Non-Proliferation Treaty, front-line antagonists — locked in rivalry or combat — begin to arm themselves with nuclear weapons.

One man representing one country cannot promise a miracle, let alone deliver one. I have absolutely no illusions about the complexity of the issues in play. Nonetheless it is essential, in my judgement, to seek stability at a number of points along the downward trend-line, and to recognize that peace and security in the modern age are indivisible.

Moreover, I am not alone. Other leaders have joined their concerns with mine. There is a growing community of political leadership which is determined to subject the science of arms to the art of politics. I draw encouragement from the support of that community.

You will know that I have just returned from meetings in Europe with several leaders of the Atlantic Alliance.... I return from Europe with clear expressions of support for my initiative, confident that my sense of urgency is shared by our friends and allies. I found a particular consensus on the need to lay down a "third rail" of confidence and communication — a rail charging our dealings with the other side with a current of political energy.

I took to my European colleagues for discussion, and for refinement in light of their own views, elements of a programme for political management of the current crisis. I return with the assurance of their personal attention to this programme. Let me set out some of the elements.

The *first* is the need to establish, as soon as possible in the course of the coming year, a forum in which global limits might be negotiated for all five nuclear weapons states. This proposal is without prejudice to the INF or START talks between the USA and USSR. But those talks, and rightly so, do not cover British, French, or Chinese nuclear forces.

What we must seek to provide is a negotiation forum for those five states which recognizes the rights of the United States and the Soviet Union as strategic equals... and which provides a mutually acceptable and stable framework for the relationship between the forces of the other three states and those of the superpowers.

In this way, neither Britain, nor France, nor China need fear that their forces will be subject to restraints which do not recognize their own national interests.

Once relative levels of armament were stabilized, I believe the five nuclear powers could begin to address the reductions called for by the Non-Proliferation Treaty, and to consider measures to control the qualitative aspects of the strategic arms race.

A *second* element is remedial action to shore up the Non-Proliferation Treaty itself — that covenant between nuclear and non-nuclear weapons states.... The Treaty has been signed by some 119 nations. But a number of key states remain aloof, including several with the capacity now, or the potential soon, to develop their own nuclear arms.

If the five nuclear weapons states could begin to strengthen their side of the non-proliferation bargain [via arms control], then the rest of us could more easily bring good sense to bear on those who have not yet signed on. No doubt we need to increase the incentives for Third World states to forego nuclear weapons — there must be a direct linkage between disarmament and development. And we shall also have to ensure that a full range of safeguards adequately governs the transfer, from all nuclear suppliers, of nuclear technology for peaceful purposes....

Those two elements begin to address the global dimension of security in the nuclear age. But we must also recognize that there is in the heart of Europe a most dangerous concentration of forces — conventional as well as nuclear. A war in Europe could destroy everything that each side desires to protect.

...The Warsaw Pact conventional forces heavily outweigh those of NATO. There is an apprehension in Western Europe that the Warsaw Pact forces could be tempted to gamble on a conventionally armed attack. They would throw down the challenge to Western leaders either of accepting defeat, or of being the first to resort to the use of nuclear weapons in our own defence.

As long as this imbalance of conventional forces persists, so does the risk that nuclear weapons would be brought into action at an early stage of any conflict.... [T]he best way to raise the nuclear threshold is to establish a more reasonable balance of the conventional forces on each side.

How then do we achieve this balance? This question prompts the *third* element of my approach. The simple, though expensive, answer is for the West to increase its conventional forces until they match those of the Warsaw Pact.... The far more sensible approach would be for both sides to reduce their conventional forces to mutually agreed levels, a task to which we have devoted the past ten years at... talks in Vienna. There is today some sign of movement in those talks, but at far too slow a pace.... That is why I explored, with my colleagues in the Alliance, ways to break the deadlock....

Another negotiating forum will open soon in Stockholm, this January [1984]. Its lengthy title, showing the complexity of its task, is the "Conference on Confidence and Security-Building Measures and Disarmament in Europe." It is imperative that this Conference not lose its way in litigation about procedures, or in the linguistics of technicality.... [W]e don't have to follow the same path with this conference, on disarmament on Europe, as we have followed with the Vienna negotiations.... I have therefore proposed that we consider the merits of *high-level political representation* at the very start of the Stockholm negotiations....

Finally, a *fourth* element in my initiative flows from the strategy of suffocation which I first proposed to the United Nations Special Session on Disarmament in 1978. That strategy — which still requires, and awaits, the support of the five nuclear powers for its implementation — needs further elaboration to keep pace with technological advances. Arms control measures must address those new technologies which, by their very nature, would make stability a more elusive goal.

I have in mind a ban on the testing and deployment of those anti-satellite systems designed to operate at high altitude. Such weapons could attack the global communications which are of critical importance for crisis management. Destruction of the other side's command and control network, at a time of crisis, would leave him blind and mute at the very moment when stability demands awareness and response, not the panic reaction of "launch on warning"....

Whether the fear is that one's communication system will be disrupted, or that one's weapons will be rendered useless, the danger is that, in a moment of crisis, the side which feels threatened will launch its nuclear missiles before the other side has a chance to strike first. It is this fear which is aggravated by destabilizing technical advances such as high-altitude anti-satellite weapons.

Neither superpower has yet developed an anti-satellite system for high altitudes. An agreement not to do so is therefore still possible. No agreement means vast expenditure by both sides — funds better spent on more worthy projects. No agreement means a further spiral of competition — a competition particularly vulnerable to accident or miscalculation. Moreover, an agreement could encourage movement toward negotiations about anti-satellite weaponry designed to operate at lower altitudes.

I am also concerned about another potentially destabilizing development, which is the possibility that new intercontinental strategic weapons may be so highly mobile as to be virtually invisible. This would call into question the ability of either side, or any international body, to verify arms control agreements. You see the paradox.... If missiles stay in one place, the enemy knows where they are, and could destroy them by launching a first strike, so that the side under attack could not respond with an attack of its own. One side would win the war simply by destroying the other's nuclear missiles.

That is why these [static] weapons are destabilizing. You must use them or lose them. For that reason, making these missiles mobile also makes them more stabilizing since, in a first strike, the enemy would not know exactly where they are. Consequently he would not start a war, because the other side would have maintained the capacity to retaliate. That would assure the destruction of *both* sides, which is not in the interest of the side which might otherwise have been tempted to launch a first strike.

But there is a further paradox in the fact that, if these missiles were *too* mobile, you could not count them, even by using satellites. And if you cannot count them, neither side could verify that the other was respecting the treaties, such as SALT I, and other agreements which might be reached.

Canada continues to devote attention, and resources, to problems of verification which must be resolved if arms control measures are to be durable and trusted. We believe that the prospects for arms control would be considerably enhanced if the verification factor were taken into account in the *developmen-*

tal stage of any new strategic system — rather than leaving it to the point where systems are put on the bargaining table.

It is therefore my intention to introduce, at the appropriate time and in the appropriate disarmament forum, papers calling for international agreement (a) to ban the testing and deployment of high-altitude anti-satellite systems; (b) to restrict excessive mobility of ICBMs; and (c) to require that future strategic weapons systems be fully verifiable by "national technical means." That is to say, that the space satellites of each side can see what is being prepared, constructed, and developed on the other's territory.

These are measures of substance, often technical in their detail. But if we can generate a political impulse toward a five-power nuclear conference, toward renewed political commitment to the Non-Proliferation Treaty, toward action at the MBFR talks to balance conventional forces and to raise the nuclear threshold in Europe, toward a restriction of qualitative developments in strategic technology, and toward their verification, then we could have motivated a truly global and comprehensive approach to the crisis of peace and security....

...I return from Europe profoundly encouraged by the extent to which my purposes are shared by a community of other leaders. Therefore I would like to confirm tonight my intention to travel to Japan, to consult Prime Minister Nakasone in Tokyo.... My visit there will bear witness to the indivisibility of global security in the nuclear age.

I can also announce that, in addition to the consultations under way with the United States, I have initiated consultations with the Soviet Union and with China — two nuclear powers upon which much depends.

I look forward to taking an active part in the discussion of peace and security issues at the New Delhi meeting of Commonwealth Heads of Government.... I look forward in particular to consultations with Prime Minister Indira Gandhi on the matter of non-proliferation, and on her perspective, as current chairman of the Council of Non-Aligned Nations, on the linkage between disarmament and development.

I am encouraged by this momentum, and heartened by the response. But I am also well aware that critics of my initiative have difficulty in grasping this step-by-step approach. Some would prefer the passionate embrace of an unattainable ideal. Others are paralyzed by the complexities of the issues in play. I believe that peace must be waged steadily, with caution and with realism. We must work with due respect for the fragility of political trust, for the importance of building carefully, for the need to search out common ground on which to stand.

The imperative of political action is made all the more urgent by the pace of conflict and confrontation, which threatens to overtake our ability to understand what is happening, and our capacity to manage it.

Let me remind you that when Alfred Nobel invented dynamite in 1867, he believed that the prospect of its military application was so awesome that governments would be forced to live in peace. And yet today we have long since lost the ability to comprehend the force of a nuclear blast in terms of any comparison with traditional explosives.

Peace and security are not cold abstractions. Their purpose is to preserve the future of mankind, the growth of the human spirit, and the patrimony of our planet.

The choice we face is clear and present. We can without effort abandon our fate to the mindless drift toward nuclear war. Or we can gather our strength, working in good company to turn aside the forces bearing down on us, on our children, on the Earth.

As for me, I choose to move forward, and I know I do so with your support.

DOCUMENT

EXCERPTS FROM A SPEECH FROM THE THRONE: CANADA'S ROLE IN SEEKING WORLD PEACE

OTTAWA, DECEMBER 7, 1983

...Thirty-five million people have been killed in wars since 1945, and the possibility of a major conflict is a danger no nation can ignore. In the four decades since the Second World War, Canada and its allies have sought to preserve peace through subscribing to Western collective defence and sustained efforts to resolve differences with our adversaries. Yet the current international situation is cause for considerable concern, even anguish.

The Government, in close consultation with our allies, intends to devote its full resources to exploration of every possible means to restore confidence and trust to the international scene. It will continue to advance proposals to slow the steady spiral of the arms race, halt the spread of nuclear weapons and create the conditions for greater security at lower levels of armament....

Improving the climate among nations requires knowledge, creativity, and a determination to find solutions. Reflecting Canada's concern about current international tensions, the Government will create a publicly funded centre to gather, collate and digest the enormous volume of information now available on defence and arms control issues. Fresh ideas and new proposals, regardless of source, will be studied and promoted.*

Canadians want more than ever to become personally involved in the quest for peace. The Government will increase its funding for voluntary associations and private research groups interested in security, arms control and disarmament issues. Resources for research and development of verification procedures, the basis of successful arms control agreements, will be expanded substantially....

---

* This is the Canadian Institute for Peace and Security, approved by Parliament in June 1984 and in operation by the beginning of 1985. The Institute does innovative research work on solutions to a wide range of peace and security problems, and also supports public education programs in the field through such means as conferences and films.

Chapter 5
IMPLEMENTING THE PEACE INITIATIVE

INTRODUCTION

*T*his is the longest chapter of the book, and with good reason, for it covers one of the most active and creative periods of the Trudeau era from a foreign policy perspective. It marks the climax as well as the conclusion of a remarkable political and intellectual odyssey.

Who knows what the results of Mr. Trudeau's peace initiative were? Many world leaders to whom he brought his proposals were unlikely to admit any external influence on their thinking. Their personal reactions are hard to gauge, though it is safe to assume that these ranged from warm support to cynical amusement, from honest mental engagement to rather irritated toleration.

The "before" and "after" pictures are, however, clear enough. By the end of November 1984, the East-West climate was approaching record frigidity: the Soviet representatives had left strategic arms control talks in Geneva; other discussions were bogged down or plodding along fruitlessly. Commencing shortly after the round of face-to-face discussions Mr. Trudeau held with Chinese, United States, and East European leaders, the climate began to change. It took considerable additional time and major changes in the Soviet Union, notably the selection of Mr. Gorbachev as leader, to make arms control proposals a matter for competitive bidding between the superpowers. But the *tone* of discussions shifted perceptibly around the beginning of 1984, for whatever reasons.

Both U.S. and Soviet leaders have since repeated the statement, "a nuclear war cannot be won and must never be fought," which opened Mr. Trudeau's ten-point summation of his initiative. Action to support this belief *may* follow rhetorical commitment.

The most appropriate beginning point for documentation of Mr. Trudeau's mission to other world leaders is the Goa Declaration by Commonwealth Heads of Government, which expressed support for his initiative (pp. 85–86). In the midst of this Commonwealth meeting, Mr. Trudeau took his proposals to the leaders of the People's Republic of China, in Peking (Beijing).

Returning from that visit, he reflected on his progress in an extensive interview with Toronto *Star* columnist Richard Gwyn* (pp. 87–90).

On December 15, 1983, Mr. Trudeau met with President Reagan. He encouraged the President to communicate to the Soviet Union the message of readiness to negotiate as well as of strength (p. 91). Following this meeting were a press conference (pp. 92–95), an interview with David Hartman on "Good Morning America" and, early in 1984, a meeting with the editorial board of the *New York Times* (pp. 96–100).

In late January 1984, Mr. Trudeau was an active and rather controversial participant in a symposium held in Davos, Switzerland. There he briefly outlined the Canadian proposals (pp. 101–4) and in the question-and-answer session which followed, raised the question whether the United States would launch a nuclear war if Europe were being overrun by conventional Soviet forces. This question caused substantial controversy. Raymond Barre of France said he would never even ask such a question; to do so could end the credibility of the U.S. "nuclear shield" (p. 103).

Because of Soviet Chairman Andropov's illness, Mr. Trudeau's effort to see *both* leaders of the superpowers was stymied. He decided, as a substitute, and for its intrinsic value, to see the leaders of several East European countries instead. He thus visited in rapid succession the leaders of Czechoslovakia (January 26), East Germany (January 31), and Romania (February 1).

Of these, perhaps the most interesting results were those of the East German visit. In his press conference after the meeting, Mr. Trudeau indicated the possibility of joint initiatives by middlepowers from each alliance as a way of "making progress in some places" (p. 105).

On his return to Canada from Eastern Europe, Mr. Trudeau took part in a major House of Commons debate, presenting a progress report on his initiative. In it, he codified ten points of "common ground" or "common bond" between East and West. These later were the highlight of letters to President Reagan and Chairman Constantin Chernenko, who succeeded Yuri Andropov in February, on the latter's death (pp. 106–10).

The transcript of Mr. Trudeau's press conference after a meeting with Mr. Chernenko at the Andropov funeral in mid-February unfortunately has been lost. However, its main points are provided in a February 16 story in the *Globe and Mail* (p. 111).

Shortly after arriving back in Canada, Mr. Trudeau assessed his personal options, and on February 29, announced his retirement from political life, effective on a date mutually agreed with his successor as Liberal party leader.†

The announcement did not, however, mean that he ceased activity as a head of government. On the contrary, the pace in several areas accelerated. An extensive process of negotiation was initiated to seek an all-party agreement in the House of Commons to a resolution calling for renewed arms negotiations (p. 112). Although the Progressive Conservative party supported and added to this resolution, the New Democratic Party could not be persuaded to drop demands

---

* Mr. Gwyn is a Trudeau biographer, author of *The Northern Magus* (Toronto: McClelland & Stewart, 1980).

† He left office on June 30, 1984.

that would have destroyed its credibility among the majority of NATO members.

On June 9, he took part in his final international meeting as Canadian Prime Minister, a seven-nation economic summit in London. There he urged President Reagan to "do more" for the resumption of arms talks (p. 113).

In previous chapters, the editorial policy has been to remove only topical references and other wording which might slow the reader down. In this chapter, most items have been edited more heavily, because as Mr. Trudeau spoke to different audiences, he repeated many of the same themes and specific ideas. A major exception is the speech of February 9, 1984, during which he summed up the peace initiative, presented virtually in its entirety.

DOCUMENT

GOA DECLARATION ON INTERNATIONAL SECURITY

GOA, INDIA, NOVEMBER 27, 1983

As we meet together in India at the end of 1983, representing a quarter of the world's people from every continent and many regions, we have shared both our concerns and our hopes for international security. Despite differences of approach which affect the way we analyze and judge events, it is our perception that relationships between the world's major military alliances are in danger of becoming more confrontational. In the context of heightened tensions and a continuing build-up of nuclear arsenals, the future of civilization as we know it could be threatened. None of our countries or peoples would be insulated from that fate.

We are alarmed by increasing disregard for the moral and legal principles which should govern the conduct of states; by the degree to which the ethics of peaceful settlement of disputes is being eroded; and by the readiness of nations to resort to the illegal use of force.

At this time of crisis, we believe it to be imperative that the Soviet Union and the United States should summon up the political vision of a world in which their nations can live in peace. Their first objective must be to work for the resumption of a genuine political dialogue between themselves leading to a relaxation of tensions. We believe that Commonwealth governments can make a practical contribution in encouraging them to do so and in promoting a larger measure of international understanding than now exists.

Essential to that enlargement of understanding is the need to increase contacts at a variety of levels between the governments and people of East and West. A concerted effort is required to restore constructive dialogue to the conduct of East-West relations. Only thus can a climate of confidence be rebuilt in place of the prevailing one of fear and mistrust.

In all these pursuits, we emphasize the supreme importance of political will. We therefore welcome Prime Minister Pierre Trudeau's call for a new political dimension on the quest for international security. We support his efforts to restore active political contact to help these and other such efforts in all appropriate ways.

As Prime Minister Indira Gandhi has so consistently emphasized, the central issue in securing wider progress on disarmament is the stopping of the nuclear arms race. These are essential steps for progress in working towards a world released from the menace of nuclear weapons and their wider spread. If the resources released by disarmament were ploughed back in some measure into world development, the needs of the developing countries which are in the forefront of our concern could be significantly met. . . .

Meeting here in India, we cannot emphasize too strongly our belief that an ethic of non-violence must be at the heart of all efforts to ensure peace and harmony in the world. That ethic requires close adherence to the principle of peaceful settlement. Only by such a commitment on all sides will the world's people enjoy an environment of true international security.

Finally, we retain faith in the human capacity to overcome the dangers and difficulties that threaten the world and to secure for all its people the prospect of a more peaceful international environment. We shall work together to fulfill that faith.

EXCERPTS FROM THE PRIME MINISTER'S INTERVIEW WITH RICHARD GWYN OF THE *TORONTO STAR**

FLIGHT FROM PEKING TO NEW DELHI, NOVEMBER 29, 1983

Q. ...Are you at all frustrated that you seem to be having difficulty translating political interest into political will, that is, expressions of goodwill and encouragement into an actual concrete commitment by the various leaders you have been seeing?

A. Well, I guess we will see. There has been that expression of goodwill as you say, but my interpretation is that it is more than: "We can't go, but wish you luck on your journey." It would seem to me that the reception that the initiative had at the Commonwealth meeting and their desire to explicitly support the initiative — which I certainly did not ask for; they supported it in the communiqué but...they [also] volunteered around the table to come with me or assist me in whatever way I found useful — to me that indicated that they were willing to do more than wish me well on my journey. They were prepared to take the risks of the journey with me. As for the NATO end of it, I guess the answer to your question will have to await the NATO Foreign Ministers' Meeting in December. It is true to say that they all wished me well when I visited the various NATO countries in Europe. We will see if they are also prepared to inject their political will along with the one I am trying to inject....

Q. You stressed that [NATO] meeting in Brussels several times. Will [the Secretary of State for External Affairs] be making some specific proposal, something new at the meeting?

A. No, not anything radically new. He will be culling from his opposite numbers the answer to the questions I put specifically in my communications to the fifteen other NATO leaders when I wrote to them after my European trip saying: "Here are the things we discussed. Here are the suggestions I put forward. Time is running out. Will you be represented in Stockholm — yes or no — at a political level? And at the same time eventually in Vienna — yes or no?"

Q. Back to this question of the difficulty of the potential action, of translating goodwill into actual action. Take the five-power conferences.... Now, does it frustrate you that the other people have all said the problem lies with the two big guys, not with us?

A. Well, it does not frustrate me...because that is what I expected them to say. These powers, these three nuclear non-superpowers, have stated their views on these things. They have established policies, just like the United States and the Soviet Union have established policies. The name of the game is not just to talk to them once and see them change their mind.

The name of the game is, as I put it at the very outset, to change the

---

*Mr. Trudeau has edited these excerpts in order to improve clarity and provide additional context for the reader.

trend-line. I think these three are perhaps committing the same misperception as a lot of Canadians at the outset, who thought that I was setting . . . out to reconcile the two superpowers and to bring messages explaining one to the other. I made it quite clear at the outset that that was not what I was trying to do. So when the three nuclear non-superpowers tell me we must first influence the two superpowers, I say, "Right, and that is what I am trying to do: to influence the two superpowers, and is not one way of influencing them to put before them the kind of proposition that I have explained?"

The reaction of Prime Minister Thatcher and Premier Zhao is explained in part by an apprehension that I was coming to tell them that they were naughty nuclear powers, that they should reduce their armaments. Most of their time was spent in defensively explaining to me that it was not "fair" to come to them until I had convinced the superpowers.

It took a long while to get the message through that I really was *not* coming to the three [Britain, France, and China] to get them to reduce *their* nuclear arms. I was coming to the three so that *they* could put pressure on the superpowers to reduce their level of armaments to a level where it would be possible for the British, French, and Chinese to consider limiting or reducing theirs.*

My initiative was received completely differently when I explained it this way. I think President Mitterand understood that from the outset. That is why the French are the most positive of the three concerning the idea of the five-power meeting. But the Chinese, long before I had talked about a five-power conference, had proposed one to be held after the two superpowers had agreed to reduce by half their nuclear weapons systems. Mrs. Thatcher kept saying: "It is a great idea but it can only be used once; therefore don't force us to go to the table yet." I would answer: "That is fine, you know. I am just begging you: don't take five years to do it. Help me create circumstances where we can get the two superpowers to make enough progress — or apparent willingness to progress — at Geneva. Then you can sit down collectively." That doesn't mean the five have to meet together in January or March, but it means that they must begin exploring together the need for them to meet eventually.

Q. That five-power conference. Is it really an attempt to find some acceptable substitute for the Geneva talks?
A. No, in no sense. The Geneva talks must go on. The two superpowers must reach agreement amongst themselves. They hold ninety-five percent of the world's strategic arms. The other three only hold five percent. . . . [T]he perversity of the situation is that nobody can sort out how you can make them progress in Geneva . . . what I am trying to do . . . is to try to get movement out of those two superpowers. As I told Chairman Deng this morning, "I can talk to my NATO colleagues — I have been talking to them — but I cannot talk to the Soviets and influence them as a member of another alliance unless I have some movement from other quarters. Now,

---

*In reviewing the manuscript for this book, Mr. Trudeau noted that Soviet leader Mikhail Gorbachev has recently indicated a willingness to consider the British and French nuclear arsenals separately from those of the United States. He has also indicated a desire to reduce tensions with the Chinese.

what are you going to do, Chairman Deng?'' I leave them with the question and I hope the dynamic will work on its own.

Q. What can you yourself now do? Are you into "Stage Two," in your own phrase? Are you going to give another speech . . . ?

A. Well, in fairness, I won't be able to answer that until I have seen the reaction [of our NATO partners] in Brussels. That is only a couple of weeks away and I will see. Maybe if we are, in our terms, successful in Brussels, I will be able to go into Stage Two and maybe go to Moscow and say: "Well, look. Here is what happened in Brussels and, therefore that means that we are prepared to politicize — shall we say — the Stockholm Conference. What are you prepared to do?" I may not even have to go to Moscow. Maybe Moscow will read the communiqué out of Brussels and say, "It is obvious that we are to go, too."* Conversely, if Brussels is a failure, then I will have to go back to Stage One and start talking the thing up again. . . .

Q. In your Stage Two, the culminating points are, of course, Moscow and Washington. What is your thinking about the psychology and the practical considerations in which you go to first . . . ?

A. Well, I think it is always quite clear that I wanted to see the three lesser of the five nuclear powers before seeing the two superpowers. . . . To be quite honest, it will depend on their own timing which I see first. President Reagan has said he wanted to see me; President Andropov, that he wanted to see me. I would go at whatever date they want to see me. If I had my druthers, I suppose it would be better for me to see the Soviets first so that I could catch up on my knowledge of them before meeting President Reagan again.

Q. . . . In terms of the total span ahead of you for your mission to succeed or fail — however one defines success or failure — how long are you looking at roughly?

A. I don't think one will know whether I was successful or whether I failed until one reads future events over the next many, many months. In an operation like this, the process itself is the success or the failure. You don't have to succeed in order to try, and you don't have to win in order to fight. It is the debate itself which will or not have been started which is important.

That debate will, in a sense, take place without me or certainly without me being prime mover. It will have a dynamic of its own. That is what I hope will happen. Our peoples all want peace — that is certain on both sides of the alliance — perhaps as a result of the initiative, they will see that their political leaders are actively negotiating, bargaining, participating. This will bring a change in the trend-line. It will mean that rather than sitting back a bit helplessly as we all have been, and seeing things go from bad to worse, we will be trying to make things happen for the better. In other words, the peace process will become part of our political preoccupations.

---

*This is in fact what happened: all countries attending the Stockholm Conference accepted Canadian urgings to be represented at the foreign minister level; the first productive meeting between U.S. Secretary of State George Shultz and then Foreign Minister Andrei Gromyko took place there.

I would suppose at that stage, some other operation will have to begin. Certainly, I can't go around many, many months seeing the same people over again, repeating the same message. If it hasn't taken a visible shape of its own, someone else will have to carry on, maybe the suggestion for forming a group of nations.* Or new operations which can only be put together after this one has shown what it leads to.

Q. You said . . . that you did not see your role as being that of an intermediary between the U.S. and Russia. But, in fact, isn't an intermediary needed? I mean, the two powers are still shouting at each other and it is going to take someone to go between them, talking softly.

A. Well, I still do not see myself doing that. I don't have the skills. I don't have the taste. I don't want to waste my time explaining each to the other. I have some ideas which I think stand or fall by themselves and if the superpowers want to listen to them and say: "Oh well, he is giving us a middle way between two extremes," that is fine, but I don't attempt to do that. I try to see what is reasonably possible and preach that. I don't have the talents of a diplomat. I think that there should be some intermediaries. It is an important role. But it is not my role, nor is it my disposition.

---

* This is a reference to an initiative of leaders from India, Sweden, Greece, Tanzania, Mexico, and Portugal to call for a moratorium on the testing, production, and deployment of nuclear weapons and their delivery systems, under the auspices of the Parliamentarians for World Order.

STATEMENTS BY PRIME MINISTER TRUDEAU AND PRESIDENT REAGAN, FOLLOWING THEIR MEETING

WASHINGTON, DECEMBER 15, 1983

PRESIDENT REAGAN — The Prime Minister and I have just concluded a very useful and a wide-ranging discussion of some of the most crucial issues that are facing the people of Canada, the United States and, indeed facing people everywhere.

Prime Minister Trudeau briefed me on his recent discussions with leaders in Europe and Asia, on his concerns for world peace, disarmament, and improving the East-West dialogue. We fully share the concerns for peace which the Prime Minister has expressed. We appreciate his strong statements supporting the joint efforts of the Western allies to negotiate meaningful arms reductions and to promote dialogue with other nations.

I thank you, Mr. Prime Minister, for coming here, sharing your ideas with us. We wish you Godspeed in your efforts to help build a durable peace.

PRIME MINISTER TRUDEAU — Thank you. You have just heard the President support what is known as my peace initiative; but I think he did more than support it. I think he has been showing, through his Administration in the past months at least, that, as far as we are concerned on the NATO side, we want to change the trend-line. We want to make it clear not only that the Alliance is strong; that it will defend itself; that it will not be intimidated; but that it is also pursuing peace.

If I were to tell you, for instance, that the President agrees that we should not seek military superiority in NATO, we should seek a balance; that we do not think that a nuclear war can be won; that we think that the ideal would be to see an end to all nuclear arms — it might come as news, at least to some of the press in Canada, because we have not been hearing that.

But this is what the President said at the Diet in Japan and this is what our foreign ministers said just a few days ago in Brussels — that we respect each other's legitimate security interests. [T]his, at least in perception, is the complete change of a trend-line which I saw when I embarked on my initiative several months ago; one which was going downwards rather than upwards...There was a call for dialogue, repeated two or three times in the message and in the communiqué.

So I am grateful...that I was able to hear from the President of the United States, the leader of the Alliance, that these are not just words; that these correspond to the intention of the Alliance, and that...the Warsaw Pact can know — that we are not trying to be superior. We are trying to recognize their legitimate security interests. We just want them to realize we want to be at least equal, on balance, and that they should recognize ours. And I think this is a great step forward....

TRANSCRIPT OF THE PRIME MINISTER'S INTERVIEW WITH A GROUP OF AMERICAN JOURNALISTS

WASHINGTON, DECEMBER 15, 1983

THE PRIME MINISTER: . . . Essentially, I wanted to make sure that [the President] didn't think I was coming here to talk about technical problems, or what should be done in Geneva, and that kind of thing. I told him I wanted to talk politics. As one politician to the other, I was telling the President that many of his positive messages were getting through but that some were not. And the messages that were getting through, not only to his friends and allies but to the other side, were that he had strengthened America . . . he had increased defence forces . . . he had re-established the United States as a country that would stick up for its rights and its honour; and he had succeeded in keeping the Alliance together. . . .

So, all of those messages were coming through — and no doubt the Pentagon was hearing them — but the message of peace was not coming through.

. . . He is a tough guy; he can carry out the decisions. But the other aspects of his message are not getting through to the people, and presumably not getting through to the other side. And whether the other side is refusing to see them because they are so paranoid . . . or because it suits [their] propaganda purpose to pretend they don't hear the signals, is something I couldn't comment on; but what I could comment on . . . is the fact that when he says to the Diet in Japan that he doesn't believe a nuclear war can be won, and it shouldn't be fought, it is an aspect of President Reagan that doesn't make headlines. . . .

Q. What was his reaction? Is there a difference between your theme and the theme that he has been carrying?

A. What is your reaction to what I just said? Is it too sycophantic? Does it look as though I have been taken in?

Maybe that is not the purpose of the interview. You know, I found myself telling him that he should be communicating better — and he is the expert communicator. . . .

His reaction? I guess it is not so much within my rules to quote what the others say in private meetings like that, but I don't think I would be breaking a very deeply held confidence by saying that the President said, "Well, you know, I've got an image of" — what was his expression? — "my image is one of being warlike"; and I said, "Who do you blame?"; and he said, "You know, my Diet remarks weren't reported." And I had to say that in Canada, they certainly were not front-page news. I see them as a change. I don't think the Administration sees them as a change. They are saying that he has been saying that all along.

I would want to analyze it a bit differently in that I think politicians everywhere — not only President Reagan, but Pierre Trudeau and the whole gang of European leaders that I have met, and those in the Commonwealth — were suddenly saying: "Hey, the crisis is too near and the danger is too great. We should really try to make this top priority."

I think that has been happening. It happened slowly. It is, in reality, the politicization of the disarmament question, which maybe our various populations have brought us to. As usual, the people often send the signals and catch the reality before their leaders do.

Q. Do you have a date with the Russians?

A. No — I have a date, but I don't have an appointment....

They asked me more than a year ago to come. They asked me at the time of Brezhnev's funeral, and then they sent a message when Gorbachev came to Canada in late winter, early spring, and then Andropov, when he answered my letter on the initiative, said I was invited....

...[W]e have no idea when they will come forth with a date. Quite frankly, I don't think the people around [Mr. Andropov] have much of an idea either. I guess it depends so much on his health. But I think at some point I will have to ask myself: Well, to keep the momentum of the peace initiative, do I go to Moscow anyhow and see whom I can see? And that will be a difficult decision. But there are people who are coming up be it the Gorbachevs, or the Romanovs. Who else? I am not a Soviet expert. I don't think that question can be answered by us. We can speculate on it....

Q. [I]t is your analysis that the trend now has gone to reduction of the chances of war in the world?

A. ...I think that it is important that at least we be, and be perceived as, nations that are prepared to talk... and seek resolution of tension and conflict by exchange, peaceful exchange....

I know the results of it will at least be that the Soviets will have to stop pretending, in the propaganda war, that *they* are the side suing for peace.

Q. Just on that point, they are not in the same position with their population. They freeze all of the contacts and sit tight. The West, given the communications problems that President Reagan has and that you have discussed with him, given the political turmoil in Germany and Britain, will sooner or later feel compelled to come chasing them with some more attractive proposal, with the usual Western impulse of "my goodness, this must be our fault. There is something wrong. So, we have to do more, give more for something better."

A. I would have been more afraid of that a year or two ago, but since then, we did deploy. We didn't lose our nerve. Since then, even little Canada, with its peaceful bent, has decided to test the Cruise missile....

[I]f the Alliance didn't crumble when the Soviets were talking peace and we were sounding war, why would it crumble now when we are talking peace and they are the ones who are on the defensive and made to look warlike?

Q. Sir, is there perhaps some latent implication — intended or otherwise — ... that if initiatives like yours...keep falling on rocky soil, then Canada and other such countries have some reasons to look in another context for their security, less connected to one bloc, if you will?

A. I wouldn't think so. I don't feel the dynamics of that operating at all. I do feel...that possibly if it falls on rocky soil that people will either become fatalistic or bored with the subject. You know: "he has talked about peace for a year now and nothing has happened; let's go on to the next subject."

But that we will go on to some other posture in the world? — I don't see that. In other words, to answer quite frankly, I don't see Canada, or most of the NATO members, becoming non-aligned. In some better world, we might hope that there would be no Warsaw Pact and no NATO alliance, but that is so far down the pipe I don't see much interest in speculating about it. If it comes, so much the better. But certainly not a unilateral disarmament, a unilateral disbanding of NATO. That is not in the cards.

Even if America and Canada were to become isolationist, if I had that as an hypothesis — and I don't think Europe would let us; you know, they are too close to the Soviets, too concerned with Soviet imperialism to let that happen.

... The "barren ground" thing led me in another direction. You know, in democracies we get bored with subjects. That's why we've got to strike the iron while it's hot. That is why Stockholm is important and MBFR is important, and Carrington is important, and meetings between NATO countries and Warsaw Pact countries, and Margaret Thatcher deciding that she must go to Budapest....

I don't know [that] that would have happened six months ago....

Q. ...Do you think it is barely possible that people in this town are patting you on the head and saying "Good going; great idea. Terrific philosophy. Very effective; go to Moscow," and then going ahead with a series of things closer to their hearts that have a lot of force and that really go very, very strongly against what you are trying to do...?

A. My inclination is to take the most straightforward and simple explanation. But this doesn't destroy your point. There are other explanations which may be true; but if you appeal to my integrity, as a man with inside knowledge, as you put it: yes, those things worry me....

Look, there will always be people...in the Pentagon, in the Kremlin, who believe that military superiority is the only way out and that we would be fools if we didn't research every possible technology and test it and deploy it to make sure that our side was ahead. You know, I cannot deny that that exists. I know there are people doing that and that there is probably a [group] of advisors in the Administration who [lean] heavily in that direction. But we had good knowledge all along....There was the so-called "Star-Wars" speech; and there is this work going on in laboratories.... I am saying that you are right to worry about that, but let's start worrying about things that we can do something about right now. And don't forget that when the political will is injected, you can have a whole series of successes, as existed between '62 and '75...agreements and treaties on outer space, on the seabed, on the hotline, on the ABMs, on the NPT, on the partial test ban treaty. This list goes on....

Q. ...The sense of what you've told us this afternoon, as I understand it, is that you feel you have accomplished, or that the events, the statements in Brussels and other things, have accomplished a good deal of what you set out to do by changing the trend-line of dialogue. The question on my mind is: are you satisfied with this, and are you going to continue? Or do you feel that you have done enough?

A. I am going to continue at least to Moscow, and I am going to continue, as I said earlier, to monitor the Stockholm thing. I am going to make sure that I continue at least on the ASAT initiatives. . . .

I don't think any leader can do only one thing. So, I'm not giving you an undertaking to spend as much time over the next twelve months on visiting various NATO and non-aligned leaders and Warsaw Pact leaders as I have in the past three or four months.

TRANSCRIPT OF AN INTERVIEW GIVEN BY THE PRIME MINISTER TO THE EDITORIAL BOARD OF THE *NEW YORK TIMES*

NEW YORK, JANUARY 20, 1984*

Q. . . . We understand that you have received a communication from Andropov in connection with your peace initiative. I wonder if you could tell us something about the terms of that communication?

A. Well, two very simple points. First, General Secretary Andropov says that he is supportive and encourages me to pursue it and that they are in general agreement with the thrust of my initiative. The second is that he wants to see me personally. He does not want me to see any of the other leaders. . . .

Q. How do you read or interpret the American position on what you are trying to do? Do you find it supportive or do you feel they remain polite and wish you would stop?

A. I guess some are the one and some the other. Some are being polite but barely, and some think that really the United States should move toward renewed dialogue. These are the two tendencies of the people in the White House. I guess the hawks have dominated for most of the time, but judging by President Reagan's recent statement and by Mr. Shultz's approach in Stockholm, there seems to be a willingness to let the more gentle line prevail for a while.

If you look at the President's most recent speech, and even Mr. Shultz's, there is the Manichaeistic fight within them. They want a new dialogue, but they want to make it clear that those who still hate the Soviets are not too distressed by that decision. So I just interpret their feelings toward what Canada is doing now in that light. At the outset, there seemed to be a rather cool reception. But when I saw President Reagan in December, he made all the right noises. Indeed, he had authorized Shultz in Brussels ten days before to sign a declaration using a new language of equality between the two sides rather than superiority, of respecting the other side's security interests, just as we want them to respect our legitimate security interests.

Q. Who are your major backers [among our allies]? West Germany, Great Britain . . . ?

A. The essence of what we are trying to do is politicize the debate, get the politicians involved. . . . In that sense, the major backers of this idea are the *people* in the various countries. If the people seemingly are the backers of it, it means that the politicians are going to become the backers, because most politicians like to jump in front of the parade.

Q. . . . [H]ow do you . . . activate . . . the political process of the Soviet Union?

A. . . . I think it is self-evident that the Soviet people do not want war any more than the American people want war. Indeed, they are probably more afraid

---

* Mr. Trudeau has edited his responses slightly to improve their clarity. Editorial excisions from the questions put to him are indicated by ellipses.

of war than we are over on this side ... therefore there is a real constituency for peace in the Soviet Union. Add to that the fact that many of the articulate spokesmen in the Soviet Union, some in exile and some in periods of grace, now realize that the Soviet Union has to develop more of the consumer side of its society and it cannot afford to keep up the arms race. So there is a genuine desire for peace and a genuine desire to spend less on arms. This is a constituency that politicians over there must serve. How do we reach that constituency? is what you mean. I think there should be contacts between the Warsaw Pact countries and the NATO countries as is happening in Stockholm.

Q. How would you define the success of your mission? The idea of the people just starting to talk again — is that it? — or do you have a longer-range definition of success?

A. Success is always defined, by politicians anyhow, post facto. Whatever happens is success and you declare victory and withdraw, whatever it is. In this case, I think there are stages of success. The first stage is getting political leaders involved. Political participation at Stockholm is a success. The objective of that participation by foreign ministers is to resume the dialogue. That seems to be beginning to happen at our end. So that's the second stage for measuring success. The third and real stage is whether the actions or the deeds follow the words. There are individual things that are encouraging; for example, the Chinese changed their stance even toward me — they had a very firm line on the five-power summit in Peking. Now they are not rejecting the possibility that if, as members of the Security Council, they were invited to be present or to join in some group of five nuclear powers they would consider joining. . . .

Q. Prime Minister ... do you think people you are talking to on all sides are really more afraid of war today than they were two years ago? ... If there really were a danger, do you not think that we would be talking very fast?

A. Do you know about that article by Tom Powers on when you start packing your bags for New Zealand? You are asking if I have started packing. The answer is no, but the *Bulletin of Atomic Scientists* has moved the clock forward by one minute now.* So I guess the answer to the question is debatable. In my view, the danger of either of the major powers wanting a war is probably less, because the magnitude of the destruction each can impose on the other is appalling. The danger is not from their *willingness* to have war; it is from a misinterpretation or misunderstanding of whether the other side is preparing a pre-emptive strike or not. In this sense, I would answer unequivocally: when two sides in a dispute hate each other, insult each other, and shout at each other, and when their technology is very, very highly developed, the danger is greater than when they are sitting down, talking, progressing, keeping their guard up, but trying to probe movement and trying to encourage movement.

Q. Prime Minister ... I have ... heard it said [by] Canadians that the [peace

---

* This publication has a "doomsday clock" in which the perceived danger of nuclear war is measured by a number of minutes before midnight appearing on the front cover of each issue.

initiative] is dictated by a political situation at home. What are your feelings about... these observations...?

A. Insofar as you are saying that politicization has come in the last few months, whether it has come in my heart or welled up in President Reagan's, I am happy. Maybe that is the definition of success that you are looking for. I have suddenly become politically preoccupied with the question of war and peace and so has President Reagan; so have others whose electoral deadlines are less close than ours.

Do all... the ministers of democratically elected governments in Stockholm, are they all suddenly seized with the fear of the electorate and are they therefore moving in this direction? If it is as elementary as that, so much the better. I do not think it is a bad thing that the politicians are suddenly seeing what people want: "They want peace and maybe I better stand for peace." That is what I have described as jumping in front of a parade and saying, "well, I started it." I think it is a mug's game to try and invalidate... particularly a democratically elected politician's motives, by saying: "Oh, he is trying to seek re-election," if that is what the *people* want.

Q. ... [W]on't all your pressure ultimately fall on the United States rather than the Soviet Union?

A. Yes, and it is meant to do so. We each only influence the people we can. If I were talking unilateral disarmament or something like that, then you might take the next step and say: Well, you know you are nudging your side and nudging in the wrong direction. I am *not* nudging toward unilateral disarmament. I am *not* nudging that Canada become neutral in world affairs. I stand up as a member of the Alliance.

...What you are saying is that it would be dangerous if we were all involved in a desire for peace and naïvely laid down arms; certainly I have been very careful not to suggest that. That is why I began the Canadian initiative of the past autumn by visiting the main leaders of the Alliance — and those who are called upon to deploy Euromissiles in particular — and made it quite clear that I was not questioning the two-track decision. I had to make it clear, too, in Williamsburg last June when we had this big hassle over what we were going to say about war and peace. You know there were those who said: "Well, we have to make it clear that we will not blanch: we are going to deploy the Cruise and Pershing II missiles by December if the Soviets do not withdraw." And there were those who said: "yes, we have to make that clear, but let us also say that we are going to negotiate to the very end and let us also make sure that we do negotiate to the very end."

...It is not just a question of machismo, of "we are going to be tough bloody guys and we are going to deploy because in 1979 we said we would deploy." We also said in 1979 that we were going to negotiate.... Although I am not a nuclear weapons expert, I would venture to say that the Soviets did not really need the SS-20s when they had the 4s and 5s. I guess I would go further and say that militarily speaking, we probably do not really need the Pershing II's and the Cruise missiles. But the Soviets began modernizing in the middle or early '70s; we said that if they did not undo that modernization with the SS-20s, we would start modernizing in 1983. And they said: "Well, if you start modernizing in 1983, we will withdraw from the arms talks."

Q. Prime Minister... If the Soviet position is parity with NATO, collective parity, then does not your approach enhance their posture, whereas the U.S. position [is] bilateral parity...leaving the French and Germans [sic] out.*

A. No, when I explained the five-power forum, I set forth a certain number of principles...which at least took into account that particular concern....
There should be parity between the two superpowers; that means we do not have to count the British and the French with the American warheads, for obvious reasons. They are marginal compared to the total strength. Also for reasons of political sovereignty, it is not a realistic start to say that the French will have to begin reducing. The Chinese made the same point to me. "We have just got a symbolic capability, why pick on us?"

...Neither Congress nor the President will ever say that we should be unequal to the Soviets because we have the British and the French. Certainly the Soviets will say, "we would like superiority over everybody," but they have to understand that that is not in the cards. The point is that everybody now has got the power to inflict unacceptable damage on each other.

Q. The missiles in Europe aside, do you accept President Reagan's premise that as of 1981, parity had broken down and that the Soviets had spent a decade deliberately wanting it to break down?...

A. The so-called "window of vulnerability." Look, I am not inclined to accept that. I am not, once again, a nuclear accountant, but I can't accept that the United States was in a position where its deterrents could not be used as a deterrent....

Q. But that could be said of the Russians as of, say, 1972? Yet they didn't stop building.

A. Yes, that is true and that is the danger of the arms race. And now, they are saying President Reagan is not stopping either. So he will go up one and then they will go up another....

Q. So, isn't the essential problem one of accounting? unless and until we can somehow equate each other's arsenals on some agreed definition of parity, we are never going to get anywhere?

A. An agreed definition of parity, yes. But I would suggest that the thrust should be working downward toward the parity.... I don't accept that we were in a position so inferior that we couldn't accept honest proposals for reducing on our side. As I say, the politics of it are different than the military aspects of it.

Q. But that's my problem. When you get the politicians, even on both sides, to say: "yes, [nuclear war] can't be won and therefore we might as well stop, therefore, let us have parity." Then they turn to the experts and their experts tell them...that is breaking parity, so we better match them. And then the other side says, *that's* breaking parity. So unless, between the politicians and the accountants, you get some agreed sense of what parity means, we are not going to break out of this.

A. I mean, that is the role of the politicians. And it is a godly role. They have to

---

*The reporter probably meant to say French and *British*.

make a value judgement at one point, which the military perhaps in their exactitude cannot make. Maybe what you are arguing is that at some point you have to take a chance for peace. You have to make an initiative, not only say the words, but make an initiative which will cause the other to decide whether he is going to follow that initiative now.*

But . . . where we are now, I am suggesting [w]e have to put proposals on the table. There are certain treaties of the 1970s — '74 and '76 — which haven't been ratified. There is the SALT II that hasn't been ratified. There is the answer to the MBFR Soviet position which was brought out last June or July which we haven't answered yet.† There are several steps we can take without lowering our guard.

---

*This is the strategy evidently being followed by at least one of the superpowers in 1987 as demonstrated by the Soviet unilateral test ban.

†A proposal made at the talks on conventional forces in Vienna.

TRANSCRIPT OF THE PRIME MINISTER'S REMARKS AT A QUESTION-AND-ANSWER SESSION AT THE DAVOS SYMPOSIUM

DAVOS, SWITZERLAND, JANUARY 28, 1984

Q. Three questions: First, according to some observers, the mutually escalating . . . arms race between the U.S. and the Soviets should be seen as our only alternative to actual war. It should be institutionalized rather than aborted. What do you think?

The second question . . . Is nuclear weapons proliferation beneficial for those countries which object to the military interventionism of the superpowers?

And the third question is: You know the United Nations was founded in order to make impossible the use of force in resolving conflicts. Now we have numerous military conflicts happening, all of which have happened over the last years. Is the monumental bureaucracy of the United Nations obsolete?

A. Well, the first question, as I understand it, has to do with the advantage of an escalating — ever escalating — arms race as an alternative to actually going to war. That seems to me a strange and certainly erroneous proposition. People arm themselves in order to seek security. They arm themselves because they feel endangered in some way. If you feel there is no other way to reduce your feelings of insecurity but by ever escalating the quantity of arms you have, you are really denying that it is possible to feel secure at a lower level of armament. Given the certain state of armament between two powers, if one side feels insecure, he has the choice of either increasing his arms or getting the other side to reduce his arms. . . .

It would seem to me that if enhanced security can come from either of those two propositions, the only sensible course to try to pursue is to try to find greater security at a lower level of equilibrium than at a constantly escalating level of equilibrium. That is why arms talks must eventually look for reduction in arms and not an equilibrium at a higher level.

Incidentally, that is very important to keep in mind when we are looking at future wars. Escalation of the type that is suggested in this question eventually will mean wars in outer space — or, perhaps more realistically, the use of high-altitude satellites in order to seek a military advantage over the other side. That is ten or twenty years down the road; it is what people sometimes understand by "Star Wars." It is a frightening prospect for all of us. It will be extraordinarily costly if we ever can reach that stage. It is likely to be extraordinarily destabilizing.

One of the objectives of the Canadian peace initiative is to seek suffocation of future techniques of waging war. It would seem to me that that is the only sensible direction in which humanity can proceed: not to involve ever higher degrees of technology and all the requirements of capital and ingenuity to draw resources from the progress of humanity. . . . I think that is enough on the first question.

The second had to do with nuclear wars in particular and the question was: "Is nuclear weapons proliferation beneficial for those countries which object to the military interventionism of the superpowers?" . . .

I guess . . . the feeling [is] that the more countries that have nuclear weapons, the more they will be able to decide the use and non-use of those weapons in another war and, therefore, they gain some measure of independence from the superpowers. The proposition sounds a little bit paradoxical but in fact . . . from discussions I have had with many leaders of Third World countries, this seems to be of others than themselves a little bit their view: Why should only five countries have the nuclear power? Why shouldn't more and more of us have nuclear power?

It seems a little bit absurd when you hear it for the first time, but it is linked to questions of sovereignty. It is linked to questions of status. And I think the nuclear powers all abhor the possibility of others than themselves having nuclear arms. It is bad enough that five countries have nuclear arms; if ten, twenty countries have nuclear arms, obviously the dangers of a nuclear holocaust are escalated. And yet, the five nuclear powers are not in a position to demonstrate this convincingly to the others, particularly if they are not white. There is also some racial undercurrent here: you know, why shouldn't the brown, the black, or the yellow nations also have weapons if the white nations have them?

There is something absurd in it, but the real absurdity is that the five nuclear weapon states have not been able to live up to the undertaking of the Non-Proliferation Treaty to reduce those nuclear weapons, to reduce their deadliness — though in some cases they have reduced the quantity of them. And because the five nuclear powers have not lived up to their undertaking, the others, the non-signatories of the NPT, have said, "Well, since you can't live up to your obligations, we will seek to acquire the atom bomb." . . .

It may be a way to object to the military intervention of the superpowers — not in the sense that you can defend yourself from the superpowers because you have a few dozen atomic bombs, but rather in the sense that you will be also the master of the survival or demise of the human race . . . which seems a way of cutting off your nose to spite your face, because the non-superpowers will also die in a nuclear war.

The third question was on the United Nations and whether it has become obsolete because there are so many wars. Well, the United Nations is the only game in town. It would be better if it worked more efficiently, but it is based precisely on the peaceful settlement of disputes. It has a costly bureaucracy, as the question puts it, which is applied to try and solve some of the disputes. . . . [O]n the record of its "unsuccess" in terms of military confrontation, I suppose you could say it has been quite ineffective. But one must keep in mind the very many other functions of the United Nations including, of course, the improvement of the gap between North and South and the marvelous work it is doing in the areas of health, labour relations, care of children, spreading of technology, and so on.

Therefore, I can't really agree with those who say it is obsolete. . . .

KENNETH DAM — I would like to make a comment upon an assumption in what Prime Minister Trudeau said. . . .

The misconception is that the United States has been steadily building up the number and megatonnage of its nuclear weapons. Let me say that nothing could be further from the truth. . . . The United States has reduced by one-third the total number of nuclear weapons in its stockpile. . . .

. . . I think it is important . . . that we not consciously give support to . . . a myth about the growth of the U.S. nuclear stockpile.

PRIME MINISTER TRUDEAU — I agree with what Mr. Dam has just said and, indeed, I slipped that into my answer... when I said in many instances we have reduced the number of nuclear weapons. The question is: Have we reduced their deadliness and their effectiveness? The whole reason for introducing the Cruise [missile], for instance, is to make [nuclear weapons] more effective. The reason we want to have a Pershing II after Pershing I is to make it more effective.

In the case of the 1,000-weapon reduction decided in 1979 and the 1,400 decided last October 29... we in effect — let's be candid — are withdrawing weapons the usefulness of which has ceased in great part. They have become obsolete or, alternatively, they are contrary to our own stated strategy in NATO. For instance, what has been reduced or will be reduced essentially in Germany are... nuclear weapons fired from artillery shells, and also the land-mine atomic weapons.... [W]hat has been decided is that not only are they obsolete but that they make... flexible response impossible. If you have an atomic land-mine on the eastern frontier of West Germany... [i]t means that you don't have any choice but to have early first use; therefore, we withdraw these. I think it is a very sensible and important decision, but it does reopen the question of quantity versus quality. Incidentally, it draws us into the whole question of whether NATO's overall strategy is still the right one....

Is the United States liable to start World War III because Europe is being overrun? That is why the Europeans asked for the two-track decision and that is why the two-track decision was taken. But as we know, the question that is being increasingly asked is: "Yes, but will the U.S. President really order use of an atomic weapon, even in Europe, if he knows it is going to result in World War III?" I don't know the answer of the President, but I guess one can speculate as to whether he would want to start World War III through [intermediate-range weapons] any more than he would through strategic weapons.

RAYMOND BARRE — ... But, if what you say is true, that if there is incredibility in the solidarity of the Alliance in all respects, at this time in Europe you will get neutralism and pacifism.

PRIME MINISTER TRUDEAU — I am not arguing that that should be the course. I am arguing that our strategy is not necessarily one which leads us away from that course, in fact.

RAYMOND BARRE — The problem is a problem of credibility. If there is a credibility gap, Europe is in very bad shape.

PRIME MINISTER TRUDEAU — ... Let me ask you about your credibility, Mr. Barre. Do you think the President of the United States, in answer to an overrunning of Europe by conventional Soviet forces, will want to start World War III, an atomic war? You have to believe that in order to not have a credibility gap.

RAYMOND BARRE — I will never put the question because if I put the question, there is no longer credibility.

PRIME MINISTER TRUDEAU — Which, in religious terms, is agnosticism.

RAYMOND BARRE — Have you read Pascal? "Je prend de l'eau bénite et je m'essuie."*

PRIME MINISTER TRUDEAU — It is what some would call the leap of faith, but democracies don't work that way. People are entitled to ask questions in democracy, otherwise, they will not support their governments.

RAYMOND BARRE — Je m'excuse d'être simpliste.†

---

*I take the holy water and I dry myself.

†I apologize for being simplistic.

TRANSCRIPT OF THE PRIME MINISTER'S NEWS CONFERENCE FOLLOWING A MEETING WITH EAST GERMAN LEADERS

EAST BERLIN, JANUARY 31, 1984

Q. As a result of your visit here.... Can we expect further progress as far as further expansion, deepening of co-operation between Canada and the GDR?

A. I think you can. Certainly, Chairman Honecker and I agreed that we should look at areas of agreement in the positions taken by both sides. For example...in the Prague Declaration of the Warsaw Pact countries last year, there were some positive proposals that we from NATO can and should accept, and in the same way, I believe, there are some statements made by NATO in Brussels in December which the Warsaw Pact countries can and should accept.

Therefore, we have asked our officials and ministers to work together to sort of identify the areas where we can agree, and this is what I call going beyond the invective and working positively to find areas of agreement.... I think middlepowers, like the German Democratic Republic and like Canada, can discharge their political obligations by identifying such areas of agreement and then turning to their respective allies and saying, "well, maybe we can make progress in some places." For instance...the Mutual and Balanced Force Reduction Talks in Vienna was an area where we both sought the same objectives, and we recognize that it is up to NATO countries now to respond to the proposal put forward in Moscow, I believe, last June [for force reductions].

Another example is the five nuclear-power meeting under the aegis of the Secretary General of the United Nations, since they are also the five permanent members of the Security Council...Chairman Honecker said that he supported such an initiative and he would urge, insofar as he was able, the Secretary General to proceed with such a suggestion.

So, there are many ideas that we share in common...and we have respectively undertaken to try and identify them and eventually act on them.

TEXT OF THE PRIME MINISTER'S REMARKS IN THE HOUSE OF COMMONS ON PEACE AND SECURITY

OTTAWA, FEBRUARY 9, 1984*

When the first atomic bomb exploded in a New Mexico desert in 1945, life itself changed. Man gave himself the power of his own destruction.

Never again would children be free from fear of the bomb. Never again would we parents be able to reassure them. Nor to calm our own anxieties.

A nuclear war would make no distinction between the sides of this House on which we find ourselves, between right and wrong, between rich or poor, between East or West, North or South.

Nuclear weapons exist. They probably always will. And they work, with horrible efficiency. They threaten the very future of our species. We have no choice but to manage that risk. Never again can we put the task out of our minds; not trivialize it; nor make it routine.

Nor dare we lose heart.

Managing the threat of nuclear war is the primordial duty of both East and West. But Canadians are concerned that the superpowers may have become diverted from this elemental responsibility. That they may be too caught up in ideological competition, in endless measurements of parity, in trials of strength and will. Canadians also know it would be foolhardy to expect that animosity between East and West will somehow disappear this side of the point of no return.

The experts would have us believe that the issues of nuclear war have become too complex for all but themselves. We are asked to entrust our fate to a handful of high priests of nuclear strategy. And to the scientists who have taken us from atom bombs to thermonuclear warheads, from missiles with one warhead to missiles with ten and more, from weapons that deter to weapons that threaten the existence of us all.

Canadians, and people everywhere, believe their security has been diminished, not enhanced, by a generation of work spent on perfecting the theories and instruments of human annihilation.

But technological push too often finds a sympathetic political pull. It is the leaders who decide on defence budgets and research budgets. It is leaders who must direct; it is leaders who must assert their will for peace, or science will devise ever more lethal weapons systems.

Canadian security is at stake; and Canada has earned the right to be heard, in peacetime and in war. Thousands of Canadians fought and died in two world wars that Canada had no hand in starting. We helped to shape the post-war world — at Bretton Woods, where the World Bank was launched; and at Dumbarton Oaks and San Francisco, where the United Nations organization was born.

We advocated universal membership in the international community — when it was not always popular to do so. As Prime Minister Diefenbaker

---

*Parts of this speech originally delivered in French; here translated into English.

demonstrated with respect to Cuba. As Prime Ministers St. Laurent and Pearson demonstrated in helping many independent states gain admission to the UN. And as my government demonstrated in recognizing the People's Republic of China and its right to a seat on the UN Security Council.

Canada emerged from World War II as one of the very few nations with both technology and resources to build nuclear weapons. But we had seen the terrible nature of the weapons and their work. Successive governments therefore, renounced this nuclear option, and applied Canadian skills to the peaceful uses of nuclear energy. In place of a national nuclear force, we joined with others in systems of collective security — in the UN, in NATO, and in NORAD.

Canada is a steadfast member of each of these three organizations. In the UN, we took the lead in peace-making and peace-keeping in the Middle East, Asia, and Africa. In NATO, Canada is one of the few countries to maintain Alliance forces permanently outside its borders. In NORAD, we contribute an element of priceless value: the airspace above our vast land. The United States can design its own defences knowing that for 4,000 kilometres north of them the land is occupied by a stable ally.

We take our commitments seriously. We have replaced our maritime patrol planes with the most advanced aircraft of their kind in the world. We have equipped our armoured units with the high-performance Leopard tank. We are phasing in sophisticated tactical and interceptor aircraft. We have launched a programme to acquire new frigates. All of this is the most modern equipment available. All of it tasked to defensive purposes.

We decided in 1969 that it was no longer appropriate for the Canadian Armed Forces to be equipped with nuclear weapons. We announced our intention to phase these systems out in a manner fully consistent with our commitments to our allies and as quickly as equipment replacement permitted. By 1970, we had divested ourselves of the surface-to-surface Honest John rockets in Europe. By 1972, we had completed the conversion of Canadian aircraft in Europe from a nuclear strike to a conventional attack role.

Also, by 1972, the Bomarc ground-to-air missiles based in Canada had been returned to the U.S.A. We subsequently decided to replace the nuclear-equipped Canada-based CF-101's with state-of-the-art CF-18 interceptors. Those CF-18's will carry out our air defence role more effectively with conventional armaments than the CF-101 could do with nuclear weaponry. This means that later this year we shall have rid ourselves of the last vestiges of nuclear weapons.

We have done more than look at our defences. We have addressed the causes of insecurity and instability, particularly in the Third World. East-West and North-South are the four points of the political compass of our modern age. The problems of the South cannot be solved in the absence of progress on global security. Massive military expenditures are distorting economic policies and diverting resources away from global economic development. This in turn is worsening Third World instabilities that ensnare East and West and add to the insecurity of us all.

Canadians, therefore, have earned the right to speak. They are telling us, the members of this House, as people everywhere are telling their own leaders, that the danger is too near. They want their leaders to act, to accept their political responsibility, to work to reduce the nuclear threat.

Last fall I spoke of an ominous rhythm of crisis. I drew attention to the confluence of three potentially disastrous trends — the resort to force to settle disputes, the risk of the proliferation of nuclear weapons, and the worsening state of East-West relations. I decided to practise what all seven leaders of the industrialized democracies had proclaimed last summer at Williamsburg: " . . . to devote our full political resources to reducing the threat of war."

I decided to use Canada's influence to call international attention to the danger, to try to inject high-level political energy into East-West relations, to turn the trend-line of crisis, to work at the crossroads of common interest between the two sides. . . .

THE INITIATIVE

Since last fall I have taken that message to Paris, The Hague, Brussels, and Rome; to the Vatican, to Bonn, to London, and to Zurich. I presented it in Tokyo, and Dhaka, and to the Commonwealth Heads of Government Meeting in New Delhi. To Peking, to Washington, and to the United Nations. I met with leaders in Prague, East Berlin, and Bucharest, to ensure that our message was heard in the highest councils of the Warsaw Pact.

At each step along the way, my message was straightforward. Canada was not looking for a seat at the superpower table. But our lives and our future were on that table, as were those of the nine-tenths of the world's population living outside the U.S.A. and the U.S.S.R.. We all had a right and a responsibility to involve ourselves, to press those at the table to remember their own humanity.

We proposed giving political impetus to the Stockholm Conference on measures to build confidence and reduce the risk of war in Europe. As many other East-West contacts collapsed, that conference took on importance even beyond its status as the only forum serving the Helsinki process of détente.

We insisted that both sides invest political effort to stimulate the talks in Vienna on mutual and balanced force reductions. These MBFR talks are the key to achieving parity of conventional forces in Central Europe and to raising the nuclear threshold, thereby diminishing reliance on early first use of nuclear weapons. . . .

We also proposed meetings as soon as possible of the five nuclear powers so that a forum might be established wherein to negotiate global limits and, eventually, reductions to their nuclear arsenals.

We urged action to reinforce the Non-Proliferation Treaty. Preventing the spread of nuclear weapons is in the interest of superpower, middlepower, and micro-state alike. And yet, as long as the five nuclear powers show little sign of initiating the reductions called for in the Non-Proliferation Treaty, we run the grave risk of seeing nuclear weapons spread to new regions and to old rivalries.

Above all, at each step along the way I urged political leaders to commit themselves personally; to put peace at the top of their agenda; to exercise the political leadership the current dangerous situation demands — to restart the dialogue between East and West.

I told President Reagan that the signals he was sending of American strength were being received in the East — but that a message of peace was not getting through. I told leaders in Eastern Europe that the harsh rhetoric of their declarations had guaranteed rejection of the Warsaw Pact's more positive proposals, and there were some.

Misperceptions and mistrust on both sides run deep. But I believe we are beginning to see signs of progress.

In Goa, in November, forty-two Commonwealth leaders strongly endorsed our efforts to restore East-West political dialogue and to promote negotiations among the nuclear weapons states....

I found . . . a very positive response to my suggestion that the middlepowers of each alliance could play a constructive part in reviving habits of consultation at the highest levels of East-West politics.

I gave them [Eastern European leaders] our Western perspective on the decline of détente, and on the importance of its renewal, and I listened to their own. We talked about the mixture of signals between East and West, and about the need to go beyond an improvement in rhetoric, toward acts and gestures to restore confidence and reduce tensions.

I returned with several conclusions from my talks in Eastern Europe:

— First, I was struck by the contrast between the cordial, reasonable, and non-ideological private talks, and the occasional blast of Warsaw Pact fundamentalism to which we were subjected in public. I believe this disparity underlines the importance of personal contact and private dialogue. Without that dialogue, both sides risk remaining prisoners of their own polemic.

— Second, because we were able in our private talks to strip away much of the invective surrounding key issues, I believe we were able to begin a process of exposing areas of common interest. That process will take time, but I dare hope that a new level of maturity in East-West relations is within our grasp.

— Third, if we are to reach that level of maturity, we shall have to grapple with difficult problems of misperception on both sides — blind spots and distortions, subjective errors of analysis or of judgement.

Few of my interlocutors, for example, seemed genuinely able to perceive, let alone concede, the gravity of the threat posed to Western countries by the deployment of Soviet SS-20s. And for our part, I wondered whether we in the West had not significantly underestimated the full impact on the East of the combination of INF deployment with the harsh rhetoric of recent years.

It will be uphill work to gain a more accurate perception of each other, and to gauge more accurately the consequences of our various words and deeds. From a confrontational deadlock where INF deployment must continue, and negotiations must be restored, only the "third rail" of political confidence and communication can ensure an early and constructive outcome.

In reflecting on these conclusions, and on the substance of my talks in Eastern and Western capitals alike, it is clear to me that areas of common concern and interest are beginning to emerge. Let me suggest ten principles of a common bond between East and West:

1. Both sides agree that a nuclear war cannot be won.
2. Both sides agree that a nuclear war must never be fought.
3. Both sides wish to be free of the risk of accidental war or of surprise attack.
4. Both sides recognize the dangers inherent in destabilizing weapons.
5. Both sides understand the need for improved techniques of crisis management.

6. Both sides are conscious of the awesome consequences of being the first to use force against the other.
7. Both sides have an interest in increasing security while reducing the cost.
8. Both sides have an interest in avoiding the spread of nuclear weapons to other countries, so-called horizontal proliferation.
9. Both sides have come to a guarded recognition of each other's legitimate security interests.
10. Both sides realize that their security strategies cannot be based on the assumed political or economic collapse of the other side.

As Decalogues go, this may seem modest. But I wonder, in this period when there are positive signs of emergence from a time of crisis, whether there is not sound purpose in going back to the basics. Beginning again, with a commitment to principles which can be shared. Finding a place to start — surveying a little common ground on which to stand. . . .

DOCUMENT

CHERNENKO BOOSTS TRUDEAU PLAN

*TORONTO **GLOBE AND MAIL**, FEBRUARY 16, 1984*

Moscow — Prime Minister Pierre Trudeau said last night after a 35-minute meeting with new Soviet leader Konstantin Chernenko that his peace initiative had come alive and a "political window of opportunity" had opened up....

During his meeting, Mr. Trudeau suggested there was a "window of opportunity" between now and June, the next Western economic summit. Events between now and then include the Vienna talks, the presentation of the North Atlantic Treaty Organization's political report on East-West relations, and the end of the first phase of the Stockholm talks. By June, the presidential campaign in the United States will also be in full swing....

NATO should respond to the Soviet MBFR proposals of last June, Mr. Trudeau suggested. But the Soviets would have to be positive in return....

Mr. Trudeau said Mr. Chernenko had...praised the Canadian initiative for its "usefulness and practicality."

Mr. Trudeau said he had not specifically discussed arms control proposals, but Mr. Chernenko spoke of the need to reduce nuclear weapons "significantly, in a major way...."

DOCUMENT

DRAFT RESOLUTION AGREED BETWEEN THE LIBERAL AND PROGRESSIVE CONSERVATIVE PARTIES

That this House,

mindful of Canada's place in the community of Western nations and of its enduring commitment to the principles and purposes of the North Atlantic Alliance;

recalling the efforts made by successive Canadian governments over the last forty years in the cause of international peace and security;

troubled by the state of East-West relations, by serious instability in the international security situation, by the continuing arms race and, above all, by the risk of nuclear war which threatens the survival of humanity;

(i) endorses on behalf of all Canadians the efforts and initiatives of successive Governments of Canada to build a climate of confidence in East-West relations, to re-establish high-level political dialogue between East and West, and to contribute to the vital goal of arms control and disarmament;

(ii) draws to the attention of all countries of East and West the following areas of common interest on which both sides can build in developing their relations with the ultimate objective of achieving agreement on actions flowing from these principles:

1. Nuclear war cannot be won.
2. Nuclear war must never be fought.
3. We must be free of the risk of accidental war and of surprise attack.
4. A recognition of the dangers inherent in destabilizing weapons.
5. An understanding of the need for improved techniques of crisis management.
6. A consciousness of the awesome consequences of being the first to use force against the other.
7. A mutual interest in increasing the security while reducing the cost.
8. A mutual interest in avoiding the spread of nuclear weapons to other countries, so-called horizontal proliferation.
9. A recognition of each other's legitimate security interests.
10. A realization that security strategies cannot be based on the assumed political or economic collapse of the other side.

(iii) calls for resumed negotiations between the superpowers on nuclear arms control and disarmament;

(iv) calls for renewed vigour in promoting nuclear non-proliferation among those countries now possessing nuclear technology and those which have the potential of developing non-peaceful uses of such technology; and

(v) reaffirms support for full-scope safeguards in the transfer and sale of nuclear technology to other countries.

(vi) directs the Standing Committee [of the House of Commons] on External Affairs and Defence to address the questions of East-West relations, arms control and disarmament.

TRANSCRIPT OF PRESS CONFERENCE GIVEN BY THE PRIME MINISTER AT THE LONDON ECONOMIC SUMMIT

LONDON, ENGLAND, JUNE 9, 1984

Q. Prime Minister, do I understand correctly...that in terms of the final statements issued after this Summit, if you have any disappointment, it is the lack of stress on interdependence between North-South economic issues and East-West security issues....

A. ...In East-West terms...we have obtained a special communiqué on East-West problems.* It would be fair to say that it was obtained much more easily, with less bloodshed than last year, and you can compare the difference of tone with the Williamsburg communiqué on East-West problems which was all in terms of "...We in the West are strong....and don't count on Western unity crumbling."

At the end [of the Williamsburg statement], there was this little phrase that I managed to get in: "...that we will devote all our political energies to working toward peace." Well, we have devoted, not only we [in Canada], but the NATO countries, and many others have devoted a great deal of energy to working for peace. I would just like to point out that change of tone in the NATO communiqués of December, and of May in Washington, where you see the idea of common interests being developed....

I refer you [also] to President Reagan's recent statement in Dublin that a nuclear war cannot be won and should not be fought. I don't think you would have seen these phrases a year ago.... I believe that the anxiety, the anguish of our populations in front of broken negotiations...has been perceived by the leadership of our various countries....

Hopefully, we are beginning to understand that [the people of the Soviet Union] don't want a war either. It doesn't mean that both sides are not going to push and probe, and so on. President Reagan said, in so many words, "a nuclear war can't be won." It doesn't mean that there aren't people in the Pentagon preparing for it and it doesn't mean that there aren't people in the Kremlin preparing for it....

I can't look ahead and say, "Victory. Any danger of nuclear war has been overcome." Every nuclear power is building more nuclear missiles and we already know that each side has enough to destroy the other many times over.... It is a very difficult intellectual problem. How do you begin negotiations so that both sides begin to build down, and how do you start? You can't just make strategic military judgements. You have to make some political judgements.... All we can hope for is that in our struggling, obtuse way we will find some way to begin building down rather than building up.

---

*At the beginning of his answer, Mr. Trudeau noted that there was an agreement to examine Third World debt.

Chapter 6

Reflections in Retirement

INTRODUCTION

*A*t his last major press conference, held following the London Economic Summit on June 9, 1984, Mr. Trudeau succinctly set out his plans for retirement:

> I can honestly say that my only resolve is to do nothing for as long as I can and I hope it will last. . . . I would not like to involve myself, either internationally or nationally, for a good period of time, so that when I get bored with myself — which may take a long while, you would be surprised — I will be free to pick and choose among the best offers. . . .

As has been so often true for others, Mr. Trudeau's retirement has been rather more active than he may have intended originally. He has taken a position with a prestigious Montreal law firm and has attended a few major conferences. He has visited Mikhail Gorbachev in Moscow, revisited the Chinese leaders, and made a number of statements which have been published in the press. His frequent public appearances still rate front-page attention in most Canadian newspapers. He is fondly remembered by people in other countries and, above all, by millions of Canadians. Inevitably, current political actions have been measured by what *he* would have done in such and such a situation, most often domestically, but sometimes in the international sphere as well. *He* has, however, generally abstained from public comment on the conduct of national and international affairs by his successors, John Turner and Brian Mulroney.

One of Mr. Trudeau's most cherished awards after he left office was the Albert Einstein Peace Prize, which he received on November 13, 1984. He made a major speech on this occasion, setting out his reflections on both the peace initiative and what had happened since (pp. 116–21).

Mr. Trudeau also contributed to two statements formulated by former heads of government. One, *Managing East-West Conflict*, by the Aspen Institute International Group, involved him very late in the formulation process. It was also signed by his contemporaries, James Callahan and Edward Heath of Great Britain; Bruno Kreisky of Austria; and Helmut Schmidt of West Germany (pp. 122–24).

Finally, Mr. Trudeau contributed a key section to a statement adopted by the Interaction Council in Paris on April 27, 1985. This was also signed by Malcolm Fraser of Australia, Jacques Chaban-Delmas of France, and Adolfo Suarez of Spain, among others (p. 125).

Toward the end of 1986, Mr. Trudeau took part in "Reenforcing Democracy in the Americas," a conference held at Emory University in Atlanta, Georgia. His comments as a panelist returned to the theme of how an end to poverty in the Third World could enhance the security of East and West. His sharp questions and probing responses illuminated the lack of a larger vision which could lead to peace in Central America (pp. 126–27).

There can be little doubt that Mr. Trudeau's incisive analytical capacities, substantial oratorical skills, and extensive contacts and prestige will be brought into play again in the future, selectively, but on international topics of moment and of more than ordinary fascination.

AN ADDRESS TO THE ALBERT EINSTEIN PEACE PRIZE FOUNDATION

WASHINGTON, NOVEMBER 13, 1984

I should state at the outset that I do not believe nuclear war to be either imminent or inevitable. If I thought otherwise, I would not be talking to you now; rather, I would be stocking up with canned goods in some remote hideaway, preferably in the Southern Hemisphere.

But I do believe total nuclear war to be *possible*...

[However] I believe Einstein gave us justifiable cause for hope and involvement when he stated, albeit in another context: "Der herr gott ist raffiniert, aber boshast ist er nicht" — ("God may be subtle, but he is not plain mean"). In other words, the problem of making peace more likely than war in a nuclear age may be extraordinarily complex, and the solution may be agonizingly elusive. Indeed, it may be at once the most important and the most difficult intellectual question of all time; but there is no conspiracy of nature, no diabolical force making the problem insoluble.

As a matter of fact, in reviewing the literature on the subject over the past several years, I am very impressed by the massive intellectual effort which is being directed — particularly in the United States — toward reducing the likelihood of nuclear war.... Let me just mention the Harvard group's *Living with Nuclear War*, and subsequent studies. Scholars, in and out of universities, institutes and think-tanks, moralists, both clerical and lay, military strategists, active or retired, members of the liberal professions, particularly doctors: all are contributing to a body of thought which continues to grow in breadth and in depth, on the subject of avoidance of nuclear war. That in itself should be cause for great optimism if it were not for the following fact.

On the whole, government leaders seem unwilling or unable to contribute much to the solution of the problem. I do not suggest that they are not concerned. I bear evidence to the contrary in that some two dozen heads of state or of government, over a period of 3 months, adjusted their agendas, sometimes at great inconvenience to themselves, to discuss with me Canada's peace initiative of a year ago.

Equally, 42 Commonwealth leaders at their meeting in India, with the late, lamented Mrs. Gandhi in the chair, devoted some two days to discussing the nuclear peril. And the initiatives of the Parliamentarians for World Order led to a most welcome statement by a distinguished group of six officeholders....

But this show of concern is generally sporadic, and can only occasionally be characterized as seminal. More important, it is not being translated into political action by the political community as a whole.

Compare the past ten years to the previous ten. From 1963 to 1974, multilateral and bilateral (U.S-U.S.S.R.) arms control agreements or treaties included: the Limited Test Ban Treaty, the Hot-Line Agreement, the Outer-Space Treaty, the Non-Proliferation Treaty, the Seabed Arms Control Treaty, the Accidents Measures Agreement, the Anti-Ballistic Missile Agreement, the SALT I Agreement, the Biological Weapons Convention, the Prevention of Nuclear War Agreement, the Threshold Test-Ban Treaty.

Since 1974, there has been only one multilateral treaty, the Environmental Modification Agreement, and two U.S.-U.S.S.R. Agreements, the SALT II and the Peaceful Nuclear Explosions Treaty, and both have remained unratified. But no progress on the START, no agreement on the INF Talks, no results on MBFR in Vienna, no advance in Stockholm, no movement yet on the NPT, even though the treaty is up for review in 1985.

One might surmise that such a dismal record would spur heads of government, both East and West, into action. But consider the following: for the first time since the Harmel Report of 1967, NATO attempted a comprehensive analysis of East-West relations in May 1984. And though one must welcome the desire for dialogue and the call for increased levels of security at lower levels of armaments, as set out in the report, one must sadly recognize that the report fails to deal with the Alliance's most important hard issue: military strategy. Efforts to open up that can of worms have been rejected as premature and divisive.

Alas! Having attended four out of the six Summits held since NATO's inception in 1949, I bear solemn witness to the fact that NATO Heads of State and of government meet only to go through the tedious motions of reading speeches, drafted by others, with the principal objective of not rocking the boat. Indeed, any attempt to start a discussion, or to question the meaning of the communiqué — also drafted by others long before the meetings began — was met with stony embarrassment, or strong objection. Is it any wonder that the value of NATO as a political alliance is increasingly being questioned?

Discussions of the nuclear threat among leaders at the Economic Summits are somewhat more tolerated. But the pressure to conform is every bit as strong as at NATO summits. Efforts at Williamsburg to send out a message of peace as well as one of military preparedness, and attempts in London to include on the agenda a discussion of areas of common ground between East and West were characterized as "giving comfort to the Russians"!

I cannot, of course, vouch for what happens at Warsaw Pact Summits, but having had discussions with several of the participants, I can fairly guess that the party line is adhered to every bit as much on their side as it is on ours. And I do know for a fact that a Ceaușescu's initiatives are no more eagerly welcomed over there than a Papandreou's over here.*

Meanwhile, a handful of scientists and technocrats, in their genius and devotion to what governments believe to be right, have brought the human race to the brink of extinction. In ten years, their shortsighted dedication has moved us back from the fearsome but stable balance of terror which we called nuclear deterrence, and taken us into an era of highly destabilizing weapons systems.

I relate these facts, not in a spirit of grievance, but in order to provoke reflection on a most astonishing reality: it is the political leaders in office who will decide whether the possibility of nuclear war will be transformed into a likelihood, and from a likelihood into a reality; it is they who will be held accountable for the success or failure of efforts to turn back Armageddon. Not the scientists, not the military commanders, not the arms merchants, not the negotiators; but the politicians. And yet, they are the ones who are mostly absent from the discussion and attempted resolution of the nuclear impasse. Why?

---

* A reference to the unease caused by Greek Premier Andreas Papandreou's questioning of NATO alliance policies and the proposed nuclear freeze initiative with non-aligned nations.

I had long sought the answer in terms of the personalities of leaders and the mood of nations, as influenced by their political misfortunes: Watergate, Vietnam, Teheran, in the case of the United States; the lost showdown over the Cuban missiles, the Polish upheaval, and the continuing leadership crises, in the case of the U.S.S.R.

I was wrong. The explanation lies in a much more simple paradox: the politicians, who once stated that war was too important to be left to the generals, now act as though peace were too complex to be left to themselves.

In saying so, I intend no offence to the political leaders. The subject-matter is esoteric, the literature is voluminous, replete with jargon and laced with contradictions. Any government leader who wanted to master the topic completely would have difficulty in discharging all his other duties, particularly when the difficult economic situation calls for so much attention. Hence the temptation to rely on others, be they Ministers, Ambassadors, chiefs of staff, technocrats, or negotiators. In the last analysis, this means that the nuclear accountants (as Carrington called them) on both sides hold the world to ransom. And judging by their performance these past years, the world is entitled to ask questions.

Who, for instance, aborted the "Walk-in-the-Woods" Formula — which might have brought the INF negotiations to a successful conclusion a couple of years ago? And why? I tried to find out, both in the White House and in the Kremlin, and it is a fair guess that neither leader knew the answers. The closest I came to knowing why was that the Pentagon did not want to give up the Pershing IIs. A remarkable position, since Helmut Schmidt who, as Chancellor of the Federal Republic of Germany, had asked for the Pershing IIs in the first place, has stated that *he* would have *welcomed* the Walk-in-the-Woods Formula! As for the Soviets, it would appear that their generals saw no necessity of reducing the number of *their* Euro-Missiles, if they could rely on the peace movements in the West to prevent deployment of *ours*. Thus, we are left with the bizarre result that, in matters pertaining to peace, even when the decisions are *political*, they are enveloped in such technical complexity that they cannot be taken by the politicians!

An interesting corollary of the foregoing is that — since only the superpowers are present in the [strategic and intermediate nuclear arms] negotiating chambers — the rest of us, in the East and in the West — will never know for sure how intelligently or effectively each side played its cards.

I am not implying that the various leaders on both sides play *no role at all* in their respective alliances. On the contrary, where armaments and military budgets are concerned, political will is generally quite apparent. On our side, the U.S. are developing the MX and ASATs; Britain and France are busily modernizing and increasing their nuclear arsenals; West Germany insists on forward deployment of NATO forces, thus making a policy of *no early* first use difficult to conceive. The rest of us, realizing that we are the beneficiaries of the American nuclear umbrella, do what we can to be good members of the club: some accept deployment of Euro-Missiles on their soil, some beef up their defence expenditures, Canada tests the Cruise. One way or another, we all make our little effort to strengthen the Alliance, that is to say, we all dutifully contribute to the arms race.

On the other side, as beneficiaries of the Soviet nuclear umbrella, the behaviour of the Warsaw Pact countries seems to follow much the same pattern.

All of which is to say that government leaders everywhere are very much involved in the politics of war. They are not very much involved in the politics of peace, except insofar as the adage goes: *si vis pacem, para bellum**....

This is not the place to review and assess the various aspects of my proposals and peregrinations. Suffice it to say that between East and West the shouting has subsided, the insults are less pointed, and the meetings have become more frequent and less frowned upon. Time is right for the involvement of government leaders in the politics of peace. President Reagan has been re-elected, NATO has demonstrated steadfastness by showing that it could, without splitting the Alliance, carry through with its two-track decision. The Soviets realize that they cannot modernize their SS4s and 5s into SS20s without provoking a parallel response on our side.

Having proved that it could follow through on the second track of its 1979 decision (modernization, i.e. deployment), NATO is now well placed to give the first track (negotiation) another try.

Surely in such circumstances, one ought no longer to be suspected of disloyalty to NATO for saying: *si vis pacem, para pacem.* Indeed, it is official NATO policy to seek parity with, rather than superiority over, Warsaw Pact forces, and to recognize the legitimate security interests of the Soviet Union. President Reagan has stated that a nuclear war could not be won and should not be fought. President Chernenko's recent interview with the *Washington Post* also provided a positive message.

Of course, everything remains to be done! A climate of trust will not replace suspicion without a vast reassessment of the principles guiding East-West relations. In that regard, the Aspen Institute's *Project on East-West Relations*, soon to be released, deserves enormous respect and influence [see pp. 122–24].

Economic insecurity and political instability in the Third World will also have to be recognized as one of the main causes of war. Since 1945, the world has witnessed 130 conflicts which killed some 35 million people, all of them located in the Third World. Aside from the so-far successfully managed NATO-Warsaw Pact [relationship, the politics of] East and West concentrates on developing country geopolitics: Western Asia, Southeast Asia, Arabian Gulf, Middle East, Horn of Africa, Maghreb, Southern Africa, Caribbean, Central America. Vast energies will have to be expended by the North in the South if the conditions for peace are to be created there.

I refer here to much more than economic aid. The fact of regional conflict and the danger of such conflict leading to confrontation between the U.S.A. and the U.S.S.R. stand in stark contrast to the inertia shown in recent years by the Security Council in acting to keep the peace. Restraint in the use of the veto is most urgent, in order that the carefully constructed conflict-resolution machinery of the U.N. may be brought to bear in some of the flash points I just mentioned.

Another grave obligation rests on the five permanent members of the Security Council, since they also happen to be the five nuclear powers. In their never-ending quest for security, they are actively in breach of solemn international obligations such as the Non-Proliferation Treaty. By failing to observe article six of the NPT, they are directly encouraging the wider spread of nuclear arms, and that in turn increased the likelihood of a total nuclear war caused by

---

* "If you want peace, prepare for war."

the cataclysmic use of such arms by others than the big five. I renew my call for a summit of the five nuclear powers which they viewed so cautiously when I appealed to each in turn last year. But I will return to this point in a minute.

Most important of all, NATO must be transformed into a vital political alliance, as had been intended in the beginning, and the new Secretary General of NATO, Lord Carrington, has both the intellect and the nerve to oversee such a transformation. NATO summits must be frequently held, and sufficient time must be allowed for fruitful and creative exchanges. If heads of government allow themselves to behave like the democratic leaders that they are, their thoughts and actions will soon gravitate to peace. And this is not wishful thinking. A vibrant democratic alliance will have no need for bombast or pusillanimity. Once macho posturing is replaced by self-confidence, everything becomes possible.

NATO should respond constructively to the several positive proposals made by the Warsaw Pact countries... rather than react only to the shrill propaganda in which they were couched.* In turn, the Warsaw Pact could be invited to look constructively at the Brussels declaration of... December [1983]. Carrington could put out feelers for exchange visits between the political and military leaders of the two Alliances.... NATO should do the following:

1. Declare that upon the achievement of the reduction of forces to the MBFR goals (900,000 total on each side), and given adequate verification provisions, it... will adopt a *no first use* of nuclear weapons policy;

2. Enjoin those of its members participating in the MBFR talks in Vienna to respond more constructively to the Soviet proposal of mid-1983;

3. Request of its members who are nuclear powers that they take part in exploratory 5-power talks under the aegis of the Secretary General of the U.N.;

4. Support the French proposal or the one I made a year ago, for banning the testing and deployment of those anti-satellite systems designed to operate at high altitude;

5. Announce a temporary moratorium on the deployment of INF† weapons in Europe, making it clear that it expects a reduction of equivalent Soviet weaponry, as well as a Soviet undertaking to resume negotiations immediately.

Envisaging any one of those five steps is likely to cause a flap among those bureaucrats of NATO who still believe that peace is too important to be left to the politicians. But I am convinced that many others will heave a sigh of relief that common sense is finally taking charge, and that the downward spiral of paranoia and distrust is finally being broken.

Of course, this can only happen if such gestures are matched by equivalent signals from the Warsaw Pact. *Both* sides must do their part. And so I call upon the Soviet Union and its Allies to show by similar concrete actions that they too have sufficient self-confidence to make a gesture, to take some small risk in the interest of reducing the threat of war.

[M]ankind now possesses the power to prevent... all opportunity, all life:

---

*The Prague Declaration, January 1983.

†Intermediate Nuclear Force.

the power to create a permanent winter, in Carl Sagan's words "a Nuclear Winter." In a world with untold riches yet to be discovered, with countless symphonies and novels yet to be written, with massive human wants yet to be alleviated, in this world a handful of men and women have dedicated their energies to the design of explosive power so overwhelming that the use of only a small portion of it endangers the continued existence of life on this planet. The decision to destroy the brilliant accomplishments of 7 millennia of poets and architects, musicians and scholars, theologians and artists, to destroy all of God's handiwork, to place in jeopardy the lives of almost five billion people — that decision lies essentially in the hands of two men, one in Washington, the other in Moscow.

I know them both. Neither, in my judgement, is evil. Each, in my judgement, profoundly hopes that the vicious genie contained in each of their bottles will never be released.

DOCUMENT

EXCERPTS FROM *MANAGING EAST-WEST CONFLICTS: A FRAMEWORK FOR SUSTAINED ENGAGEMENT*, STATEMENT OF THE ASPEN INSTITUTE INTERNATIONAL GROUP

NEW YORK, AUTUMN, 1984

BASIC PRINCIPLES

The undersigned have been involved in international relations for most of the atomic age. Our experiences have taught us that neither East nor West can be secure when the other is insecure, particularly with respect to nuclear weapons. There can be mutual security or mutual insecurity, but it will be mutual in either case. What can be done?

The first, inescapable requirement is to face squarely the destructive power of thermonuclear weapons.... [E]ach side's weapons ensure that the other's are not used. Each deters the other. Such deterrence, in our judgement, is neither immoral nor illogical. There have now been almost four decades of nuclear peace, in spite of serious East-West crises. But deterrence may not be eternal, and behind it there always yawns the atomic abyss....

Statesmanship can and must guide us all through this dangerous passage. Political leaders of East and West have recognized that the power to destroy involves the responsibility to conserve. A stable balance should be the goal. It alone cannot guarantee peace, nor does it fire the imagination, but it can be made to work. It is the responsibility of leaders on both sides to conserve this balance at the lowest level....

REDUCING RISKS: NO EARLY USE

The unimaginable horror of thermonuclear war should not blind us to the imaginable horrors of conventional war. A sound security policy for the West must reduce the risks of both....

We believe it is essential to reduce Western reliance on nuclear weapons in Europe. We therefore recommend that the Atlantic Alliance move toward no early use of such weapons.

One means of reducing nuclear risks deserves priority attention: the further withdrawal of NATO short-range, battlefield nuclear weapons from the dividing line in Central Europe.... The "use them or lose them" dilemma would operate rapidly during the inevitable fog of battle, and using them could initiate the march up the escalatory ladder. The possibility of premature or unnecessary use of nuclear weapons should be unacceptable to Alliance leaders and steps should be taken to eliminate it....

There are deep-seated political and ideological problems between East and West, and curbing the arms race will not automatically solve them. The continuance of the nuclear arms race, however, and its expansion into previously unexploited technological areas, will tend increasingly to poison political relations, making resolution of problems ever more difficult and ultimately imperilling peace itself. We have put the political relationship in first place, but East and West must also move forward simultaneously and on a broad front with arms control. This will continue to be a central index of progress and a principal channel for dialogue between East and West.

We believe the goals of the West, with respect to nuclear arms control, should be to maintain an adequate deterrent posture while:
— improving strategic stability;
— regulating the modernization process;
— reducing the numbers of weapons in stages;
— lessening tensions.
These goals should be reflected both in Western defence programs and in negotiations with adversaries....

Caution is called for with regard to strategic defence. The parties to the 1972 Treaty on the Limitation of Anti-Ballistic Missile Systems retain the right to conduct research on ballistic missile defence.... Decisions or actions which would run counter to the ABM Treaty should be eschewed. This Treaty is a cornerstone of strategic stability. It should be built on and improved where necessary, but not undercut.

The troubled arms control process demands a high priority. As first steps, we recommend:
— Talks should begin promptly between the U.S. and U.S.S.R. on controlling anti-satellite weapons. Observation, communication, and other satellites have made a vital contribution to strategic stability, which must not be squandered in destabilizing efforts to gain unilateral, transient advantages.
— U.S.-Soviet negotiations on reducing nuclear arms should recommence. It is important to ensure that ceilings agreed for strategic weapons are not undermined by shorter-range systems. All of their systems capable of striking the territory of European states should therefore be addressed. A basic objective should be sharp reductions in warhead levels, perhaps through annual percentage cuts, and the gradual de-mirving of both forces.*
— Confidence-building measures from the Atlantic to the Urals are being stressed in the Stockholm Conference on Disarmament in Europe (CDE). If they have real content such measures can help reduce the risk of nuclear war....
— Previously-negotiated U.S.-Soviet agreements on nuclear testing should be brought into force and the trilateral U.S./U.K./U.S.S.R. talks on a Comprehensive Test Ban should be resumed. The groundwork for a sound, verifiable ban has already been laid....
If East and West move on these lines to restart arms control, they will be better

---

* "De-mirving" refers to removal of multiple warheads and return to single warheads for each missile.

placed to carry forward the vital task of preventing the spread of nuclear weapons. We strongly endorse the Treaty on the Non-Proliferation of Nuclear Weapons which has served the world well since its signature sixteen years ago. It...deserves to be strengthened. Further development of the inspection arrangements carried out by the International Atomic Energy Agency is most desirable. Avoiding proliferation clearly is an interest shared with the East, and with leading neutrals and non-aligned nations as well....

DOCUMENT

INTERACTION COUNCIL: EXCERPTS FROM A FINAL STATEMENT ADOPTED AT THE THIRD SESSION

PARIS, APRIL 25-27, 1985

PEACE AND SECURITY

...The arms race is a consequence of the profound differences between, and perceptions of, the superpowers. The roots of such problems can only be addressed at the political level. We assert that possession of nuclear weapons and the growing nuclear and conventional arms race pose that greatest danger to human existence. *The Council strongly urges the U.S.A. and the U.S.S.R. to identify areas of commonality which exist even in the arms field and on which further agreements could be based.* For example, both sides should *jointly* state that they agree that:
— nuclear war cannot be won and should not be fought;
— equilibrium should be sought at lower levels of armaments;
— less money should be spent on armaments;
— stabilizing weapons should be preferred to destabilizing ones;
— they seek equality rather than superiority of forces;
— they respect the other side's legitimate security interests.
To instill greater confidence in the Geneva negotiations, we recommend that the major nuclear powers commit themselves to a total test ban during the period of talks.... In addition, *the Council urges the superpowers in the strongest possible terms to attach the highest priority to the Geneva process so that constructive results, which the world looks for, are forthcoming....*

EXCERPTS FROM REMARKS DELIVERED NOVEMBER 1986 TO A CONFERENCE ON "REENFORCING DEMOCRACY IN THE AMERICAS"

EMORY UNIVERSITY, ATLANTA, GEORGIA
NOVEMBER 18, 1986*

What if the most important, most vital, most urgent question in Central America, or for that matter, in most of the Caribbean and Latin America — what if that question is *not* the form of government? What if the most important thing... is the fact of poverty?... What can the outside nations, countries, influences do to assist the transition and the strengthening of democracy?

If poverty is the priority... it would make a difference in the way outside help is brought to bear on any situation in the hemisphere. [I]f the first priority is to alleviate poverty, then it would be clear that democracy is a means, and not an end in itself.... I guess there also is a question of pace of change. Some sovereign nations don't choose to... "purchase the loyalty of the bourgeoisie," and they may pay a price for that. But surely they have a right *not* to pay that price.

My own predecessor... Louis St. Laurent, who was a Liberal — but a more conservative Liberal than some of us — ... used to look with equanimity at the socialist party in Canada and say, "Well, they're just liberals in a hurry."

[S]upposing this distinction I'm making between ends and means... permits [Nicaragua] Vice-President [Sergio] Ramirez's government to seek to tackle the problem of poverty in his country by some other means than liberal democracy. Perhaps even social democracy. After all... liberal democracy generally postulates capitalism as its economic system.

But capitalism doesn't do all that much in Somoza's Nicaragua to alleviate the problem of poverty, or for that matter, in former president Fulgencio Batista's Cuba. And Marxism is a dirty word for us. Capitalism is a dirty word in some of those countries because they find that it hasn't solved the problem of abject poverty... if they are sovereign nations, I don't see what gives us any right in international law to decide that they're wrong. Because we don't like Marxism, or in some cases, democratic socialism, does that give us the right to intervene with armed force in another country? To invade it? And how does the breaking of international law, which unilateral intervention can constitute... educate the country or continent in the ways of democracy, which after all, is supposed to be based on the rule of law?...

I don't want to get too far into the subject of intervention; there is an alternative. There is the Contadora Group's proposal and its support by the overwhelming majority, if not the totality, of the democratic countries of the Western Hemisphere, of South America. There is an answer and it comes from countries who... have made such strides toward becoming democratic.

---

* Mr. Trudeau was a panelist commenting on a series of papers presented by experts on the theme of what outsiders could do to strengthen democracy in Central and South America. These remarks were originally published in the *Toronto Star*, Thursday, December 4, 1986.

Here is an alternative which doesn't cost the U.S. treasury anything. It's something that the people of the region want to do by themselves, for themselves. And certainly not people who agree that Marxism is the best form of government. They're prepared to look for...a peaceful solution....

Surely now we should think twice before insisting that that area become a cockpit for the contentions between the superpowers. I'm not inclined to say that one is wrong, the other is right and one started and the other continued. There is an alternative solution to armed intervention. I don't see how for the life of us, if we believe in democracy, freedom and self-determination, how we don't give that alternative our overwhelming support.

I suspect that the evidence is...that the White House at this time wants to get rid of the Sandinistas at all cost. If that is not the case, well, I beg to understand some of [the U.S. Administration's] actions. [I]f...there was an intervention, as there has been in Central America at various times over the past century, regardless of who would win such a situation, it's certain that all of Latin America would lose.

...I think what is asked of politicians in this hemisphere is to exercise statecraft, to look at the problems, to see that Nicaragua, or El Salvador, are really of minimum importance when you consider their size and place in the whole of Latin America.... The big problems are elsewhere....

The big question is how is the United States and all the rest of us in this hemisphere — Canada, the Caribbean, South America, Central America — how are we going to enter the twenty-first century? Will it be with recrimination and distrust and perhaps even bloodshed? Or will it be through the exercise of high politics...which is certainly the way of co-operation, the way of constructive engagement?

Conclusion

Summing Up the Trudeau Achievement

Human history becomes more and more a race between education and catastrophe.
H.G. WELLS, *THE OUTLINE OF HISTORY**

*I*f a single motive sums up the international peace and security efforts of Pierre Elliott Trudeau, it is probably that he sought to *educate* his fellow citizens, leaders of other countries, and himself.

This motive is evident in his early efforts to make Canadians see their own self-interest as entwined in the interests and actions of other countries. It is clear in his unique access to superpower leaders to seek the best from them and occasionally to chide them ruefully. And it is apparent from his travels abroad, during which he immersed himself in the mentalities of others and participated, if only briefly, in other ways of seeing things. If there was periodic tension in the Canadian or the world "classroom" about international affairs, it was often because we or they were being pushed by the instructor.

Mr. Trudeau's major concerns were admittedly "domestic": maintaining the Canadian federation, strengthening individual liberties, and responding to fresh waves of social and economic change. As a result, some of his critics have accused him of being a "dilettante" in foreign affairs. The chronology at the end of this book shows that, indeed, his level of activity waxed and waned. But what leader of a modern democratic nation passing through a series of crises and recessions *did* pursue foreign policy to the exclusion of priorities at home? Mr. Trudeau observed as we worked on this book that he felt he had addressed the toughest international issues, but could not address them all the time.

Other critics of Mr. Trudeau's say he spent *too much* time on international matters, when the country urgently needed his attention on employment, inflation, technological change, and other "bread-and-butter" issues. These critics, however, might also be those prone to take a "little Canada" view of the world, assuming that problems can be resolved by repeated local applications of emotive attention by the leader.

---

*Jonathan Green, ed., *The Book of Political Quotes* (New York: McGraw-Hill, 1982), p. 92.

The truth is most likely close to what Mr. Trudeau said of Canadians as a whole on February 9, 1984: that he saw the crisis and did what he could.

Despite many competing demands and frustrations, Pierre Trudeau followed his own compass. He pursued the idealism of the peace initiative in the face of "realpolitik" cynics. He called for actual progress on nuclear arms reductions when "pipsqueaks in the Pentagon" would rather have had a "good ally." He criticized NATO meetings for being limited to prepared communiqués and set speeches. He injected his own charisma and sense of urgency into session after session of international conferences and discussions, returning often to peace and security themes.

He did what he could, given Canada's position in the world, not perfectly, but with an understanding that some independent observers have called unique among Western leaders.*

Apart from many workaday agreements and events in which Canada played a role to be expected of any middle power, the Trudeau Government's accomplishments in promoting international peace and security include:
— ending the nuclear role of the Canadian Armed Forces;
— recognizing China, paving the way for American efforts in the same direction;
— creating the Canadian Institute for International Peace and Security, and programmes for arms control verification and disarmament education;
— strengthening of Canadian safeguards on the export of nuclear technology for peaceful purposes;
— offering Canadian Forces participation in new peace-keeping roles in the Middle East;
— upgrading Canadian Forces equipment: new patrol and fighter aircraft; new tanks and rifles; new frigates.

Some initiatives to which Mr. Trudeau was most committed personally have yet to bear much, if any, fruit: his proposals for nuclear suffocation, for a five-power summit, for an end to military exploitation of space, for "common ground" between East and West have been rejected or adopted only to a very limited degree.

However, history may yet show who had the better grasp of political "realities": those who preferred to maintain the status quo, or those who, like Pierre Elliott Trudeau, risked seeming naïve by saying things had to change and applying their political talents to that end.

United States historian Lee Simonson says: "Any event, once it has occurred, can be made to appear inevitable by a competent historian."† The history of the Trudeau era in retrospect may be made to fit into categories of inevitability: he did thus and so because of American pressure, or because he had to defend Canada's national interests, or because he enjoyed meeting other leaders. We should avoid falling into this trap. Perhaps this book of readings has helped make it clear that, amid the inevitable compromises and missed oppor-

---

*In discussions about this book, Mr. Trudeau paid tribute to the quality of his advisors, most professional public servants, such as Ivan Head, Robert Fowler, Maurice Archdeacon, and others who taught him the details and made his work so much easier.

† *Ibid.*, p. 204.

tunities, there were startling innovations and penetrating observations which otherwise would *not* have occurred.

Finally, something should be said about Mr. Trudeau's difficult role in bringing Canada through its own domestic crisis of peace and security in 1970; its commitment to allowing democratic dissent — even to the very existence of the country — survived, battered but intact.*

Given the 20-20 vision of hindsight, Canada's triumph as an island of civility and calm neighbourliness also looks inevitable and belies deeply felt struggle. Other leaders in Mr. Trudeau's shoes *might* have done as much in this regard. But *he* did it with such stubborn intelligence and unequivocal élan.

---

*See page 132 for the major events of the "FLQ Crisis" in Quebec of October 1970.

Select Chronology*

1968

APRIL 4   Rev. Dr. Martin Luther King killed by a sniper in Memphis, Tennessee.

6   Pierre Elliott Trudeau is elected Leader of the Liberal Party of Canada.

20   Trudeau sworn in as Prime Minister of Canada.

23   Trudeau dissolves the 27th Parliament and calls election for June 25.

MAY 13   Trudeau proposes recognition of the People's Republic of China and economic aid for South Vietnam as part of the election platform of the Liberal party.

29   Trudeau issues 10-page foreign policy statement including proposals for: expanded ties with French-speaking countries, a ministerial mission to Latin America, a review of Canada's relations with Europe and NATO, creation of the Canadian International Development Agency, creation of an international development research centre.

JUNE 5   U.S. Senator Robert F. Kennedy assassinated.

25   Liberal party wins 154 of the 264 seats in the House of Commons.

JULY 22   Canada signs treaty preventing it from making or acquiring further nuclear weapons: "Nuclear Non-Proliferation Treaty."

AUGUST 21   Soviet Union invades Czechoslovakia.

22   Canada joins six other U.N. Security Council members in sponsoring resolution calling for immediate withdrawal of Soviet troops from Czechoslovakia.

SEPTEMBER 12   Speech from the throne opening the 28th Parliament confirms plan for International Development Research Centre, and for review of Canada's foreign policy.

1969

FEBRUARY 10   Canada begins negotiations to recognize People's Republic of China via Canadian embassy in Stockholm.

MARCH 17   Trudeau tells House of Commons that U.S. had not con-

---

*Chronology developed from *Canadian News Facts*.

sulted Canada on deployment of a new "Safeguard" Anti-Ballistic Missile system near Canadian border.

APRIL 3 Trudeau announces new Canadian defence policy, including a "phased reduction" of Canadian troops in Europe but continued commitment to NATO; increased emphasis placed on protection of Canadian sovereignty.

MAY 23 Trudeau says he hopes neither the U.S. nor the Soviet Union will proceed with construction of a ballistic missile defence system.

OCTOBER 2 U.S. detonates 1.2-megaton thermonuclear device under Amchitka, Alaska, despite strong Canadian protests.

23 Speech from the throne announces higher priority to be given to arms control, particularly to verification of nuclear tests.

1970

JUNE 25 White Paper on Foreign Policy is tabled in the House of Commons by Secretary of State for External Affairs Mitchell Sharp; it seeks pragmatic foreign policy which serves Canadian national objectives.

OCTOBER 5 British Trade Commissioner James Cross kidnapped by Front de Libération de Québec (FLQ) members from his home in Montreal.

10 Quebec Minister of Labour Pierre Laporte kidnapped from in front of his home by two masked gunmen.

13 External Affairs Minister Mitchell Sharp announces that Canada and People's Republic of China will exchange diplomats and that Canada will vote fc: the entry of China into U.N. later in year.

16 War Measures Act proclaimed.

17 Trudeau addresses the nation.

18 Pierre Laporte's dead body discovered.

19 House of Commons approves invocation of War Measures Act.

NOVEMBER 2 Public Order Act replaces War Measures Act.

Canada tightens ban on arms sales to South Africa.

DECEMBER 3 Trade Commissioner James Cross freed in Montreal; his kidnappers fly to Cuba.

1971

MAY 18-28 Trudeau leads delegation to Soviet Union and signs protocol for co-operation in economic, scientific, and cultural spheres; concluding communiqué says both countries agreed on need for reduced armed forces in central Europe.

AUGUST 24   White Paper on Defence Policy published, announcing that Canada will get rid of nuclear-tipped Bomarc missile squadrons.

1972

FEBRUARY 14   Canada recognizes Bangladesh, formerly East Pakistan.

21   Canada accepts international verification of its nuclear development program by International Atomic Energy Agency, first "near-nuclear" state to do so.

SEPTEMBER 1   Parliament dissolved.

OCTOBER 30   Liberals fail to win majority of seats in General Election.

NOVEMBER 2   Recounts give Liberals 109 seats to 107 for the Progressive Conservatives; Trudeau announces he will try to govern with minority.

22   Trudeau names new Cabinet.

DECEMBER 22   External Affairs Minister Sharp announces Canada ready to begin talks leading to official recognition of East Germany.

Former Prime Minister Lester B. Pearson dies in Ottawa.

1973

JANUARY 4   Speech from the Throne expresses Canadian support for talks on European security and co-operation, for strategic arms limitation talks between U.S. and U.S.S.R., and for mutual and balanced force reductions.

5   Government resolution deploring U.S. air attacks on the Hanoi-Haiphong area of Vietnam and urging end to such raids passed in House of Commons with all-party support.

29   Canada's first members of cease-fire supervisory commission arrive in Saigon, following the Paris peace treaty announced January 23.

FEBRUARY 7   Canada formally recognizes government of N. Vietnam.

MAY 29   External Affairs Minister Sharp announces that Canada will withdraw from International Commission of Control and Supervision by July 31 after attack on helicopters carrying Canadian observers in Vietnam and other difficulties in investigating truce violations.

JULY 4   Canada proposes 5-point plan for removal of obstacles to human freedom at European security conference in Helsinki.

1974

MAY 9   Parliament dissolved following defeat of Liberals on proposed budget; election to be held July 8.

22   Canada suspends all nuclear aid to India after nuclear device detonated there on May 18.

JULY 8   Liberals win majority.

AUGUST 9   Richard M. Nixon resigns as President of the U.S. following "Watergate" scandal; Vice-President Gerald R. Ford sworn in as President.

DECEMBER 20   Tougher policy on safeguards regarding nuclear technology sales abroad is announced.

1975

APRIL 24   Canada closes Embassy in Saigon.

25   Canada recognizes Royal Government of National Union in Cambodia, following Khmer Rouge victory over previous government April 16.

MAY 1   Changes in structure of NORAD announced, bringing Canadian air defence under complete Canadian control for first time since agreement signed in 1958.

15   Canada announces recognition of new government of South Vietnam following takeover by "Provisional Revolutionary Government" April 30.

AUGUST 1   Trudeau signs Helsinki agreement formalizing post-war boundaries of Europe along with leaders of 34 other countries. Announces that Canada and East Germany have established diplomatic relations.

1978

MAY 23   Trudeau announces end to all Canadian foreign aid to Cuba in disapproval of that country's role in Angola.

26   In first speech to U.N., Trudeau calls for "suffocation" of nuclear arms race at laboratory-development stage; also calls for comprehensive test ban, halt on testing of vehicles for nuclear weapons, halt to production of fissionable material, and accord on limiting spending for new systems.

30   Trudeau calls for NATO to develop new disarmament proposals at two-day NATO summit meeting in Washington.

JUNE 20   U.N. General Assembly reaches consensus on final document on disarmament, incorporating main points of Trudeau's "strategy of suffocation."

1979

MARCH 26   House of Commons dissolved for general election on May 22.

MAY 22   Progressive Conservatives elect 136 members of 282-seat House of Commons, enough to form minority government. 114 Liberals elected, drop from 141 in previous election.

JUNE 4   Trudeau resigns as Prime Minister and Joe Clark sworn in.

NOVEMBER 21   Trudeau announces resignation as Leader of the Liberal Party of Canada, to take effect March 1980 following leadership convention in Winnipeg.

DECEMBER 13   Progressive Conservative minority government defeated by vote of 139–33.

14   General Election called for February 18, 1980.

18   Trudeau announces acceptance of draft of Liberal caucus and will remain as Leader for General Election.

1980

FEBRUARY 18   Liberal party wins majority of the seats in the House of Commons, 146 to 103.

MARCH 3   Trudeau sworn in as Prime Minister following resignation of Clark and his Government.

APRIL 14   Throne Speech promises active Canadian role in promoting disarmament and that Ambassador for disarmament will be named.

DECEMBER 13   Trudeau rejects statement by NATO Secretary-General Joseph Luns threatening Western responses to Soviet intervention in Poland, because this would simply increase tensions and give "the other camp the pretext" to intervene militarily.

1981

JUNE 15   Trudeau starts two-day House of Commons debate on foreign affairs by saying "an arms race while millions die of hunger is a veritable scandal."

1982

JANUARY 31   Trudeau calls for end to martial law in Poland during "Solidarity Day" telecast from U.S.

MAY 16   Trudeau calls for West to negotiate arms control and disarmament with Soviet Union in address at Notre Dame University, South Bend, IN.

JUNE 10 Trudeau says NATO summit in Bonn, W. Germany, did not discuss real issues such as strategy for dealing with Soviet Union or approaches to disarmament. As honorary chairman of Summit, Trudeau said no issue should take precedence over need to avoid nuclear annihilation.

18 Trudeau says U.S.S.R. and U.S. must give undivided attention to reducing nuclear stockpiles, without political preconditions, in speech to the U.N. Special Session on Disarmament.

1983

JANUARY 10 Trudeau says January 5 set of Warsaw Pact peace proposals should not be rejected out of hand, especially reduction of Soviet SS-20 missiles and no-first-use commitment on conventional as well as nuclear forces.

FEBRUARY 10 External Affairs Minister Allan MacEachen announces agreement signed which will allow U.S. testing of weapons systems in Canada.

APRIL 28 Trudeau meets President Reagan and indicates support for "two-track" policy in Europe: deploying new nuclear weapons to counter Soviet deployment but also pursuing negotiations for mutual reductions.

MAY 4 Trudeau welcomes Soviet proposal to reduce medium-range nuclear weapons in Europe, and urges President Reagan to have summit meeting with Soviet leader Yuri Andropov.

14 Trudeau says suggestions the U.S. could win nuclear war are "pretty absurd" in *Toronto Star* interview.

30 Trudeau able to secure references in communiqué following 7-nation Williamsburg Summit, which pledges leaders "to devote [their] full political resources to reducing the threat of war."

JULY 15 Cabinet decision to approve testing of unarmed Cruise missile in Canada announced.

SEPTEMBER 1 Korean Airlines Flight 007 to Tokyo shot down over Sea of Japan by Soviet fighter, killing all 269 aboard, including 10 Canadians.

12 Canadian House of Commons unanimously condemns Soviet actions re KAL 007.

OCTOBER 27 Speaking at conference in Guelph, Ontario, Trudeau calls for "jolt of political energy" to be injected into arms negotiations and puts forward five-point plan for reducing nuclear tensions.

NOVEMBER 11   Trudeau returns from mission to Europe during which he brought proposals for reducing nuclear tensions to key NATO leaders.

13   Trudeau reports on results of European mission in Montreal luncheon speech; mentions more specific elements of his proposals, including ban on high-altitude anti-satellite weapons systems and agreement to restrict "excessive mobility" of ICBMs.

15   Senior U.S. State Department official, Kenneth Dam, says Reagan administration welcomes Trudeau "peace initiative" but disagrees that political will to pursue arms control lacking in Washington.

27   Commonwealth leaders sign declaration calling for U.S. and U.S.S.R. to resume arms talks, and endorse Trudeau's peace mission.

28–29   Trudeau meets with Zhao Ziyang, Prime Minister of People's Republic of China, and with Deng Xiaoping, top leader, regarding his peace proposals.

DECEMBER 7   Throne Speech stresses dangers in East/West relations and proposes centre to study proposals for arms control, disarmament, defence, and conflict resolution as well as other Canadian steps to support drive for peace.

8   NATO foreign ministers agree to send high level representation to 35-country conference on confidence-building measures to be held in Stockholm, January 1984.

14   Church leaders meet Trudeau in Ottawa and support peace initiative.

15   Trudeau meets President Reagan, who wishes him "Godspeed in your efforts to help build a durable peace," but does not endorse specific proposals.

1984

JANUARY 3   Chinese Premier Zhao Ziyang expresses support for Trudeau peace initiative.

10   Canadian Third Track for Peace group, non-partisan committee of academics, writers, and scientists, meets Trudeau in Ottawa and supports initiative.

11   Trudeau visits U.N. Secretary General Javier Perez de Cuellar asking that U.N. serve as forum for five-power arms-reduction negotiations.

25   Trudeau meets leaders of Czechoslovakia to discuss peace proposals.

28   Trudeau suggests that NATO strategy of relying on first use of nuclear weapons may not be credible, during discussion in Davos, Switzerland.

30–31   Trudeau visits East German leaders.

FEBRUARY 1   Trudeau visits Romanian leaders.

9   Trudeau reports on results of peace initiative in major speech to House of Commons; sets out 10 points of "common ground" between East and West.

15   Trudeau meets new Soviet leader Constantin Chernenko following funeral of Yuri Andropov.

29   Trudeau announces he will retire as leader of Liberal party after new leader selected.

MAY 15   Announced that Trudeau has written to President Reagan and Constantin Chernenko proposing renewed effort at nuclear arms control; efforts to have a 3-party resolution in House of Commons fail.

31   NATO foreign ministers issue 13-point statement on East-West relations following talks in Washington.

JUNE 8   Seven-nation economic summit meeting in London approves special declaration on East-West relations and peace, based on draft circulated by Trudeau.

14   Trudeau speaks to Liberal party leadership convention following tribute to him. Notes that sometimes is a need to speak to people directly, "over the heads of the superpowers."

27   Announced in Washington that Trudeau has won Albert Einstein peace prize.

29   Royal assent given to Bill C-32, act to establish Canadian Institute for International Peace and Security.

30   Trudeau resigns officially; new Liberal Leader John N. Turner sworn in as Prime Minister.

Bibliography

This bibliography is intended as a guide to English-language readers who would like to read more about the foreign policy and international relations of the Trudeau era. For researchers, it provides detailed references for many items contained in the foregoing text as well as an indication of the full scope of Mr. Trudeau's policy statements.*

Part A is a selected and annotated list of books which place the Trudeau era in perspective. They contain critical assessments of his work and also theoretical frameworks for understanding why Canada took the positions it did between 1968 and 1984. Part B is a list of Mr. Trudeau's own publications in the foreign policy field, taken from the External Affairs Department's documentation series and from available bibliographies. Part C is a list of other published bibliographies which cover the Trudeau era in whole or in part.

A: BOOKS ON THE TRUDEAU ERA IN INTERNATIONAL RELATIONS

Blanchette, Arthur E., ed. *Canadian Foreign Policy, 1966–1976: Selected Speeches and Documents.* Toronto: Gage, 1980.

This is the most recent in a series of edited foreign policy documents published in the "Carleton Library." It includes materials from the House of Commons debates, *Statements and Speeches* published by the Department of External Affairs, the *Canada Treaty Series*, other government publications, and press releases. Each chapter is prefaced by a two- or three-page introduction by the editor. Subjects covered include: the United Nations, NATO, Canada-United States relations, the Far East, the Commonwealth, international economic policy, international development, the environment, and the role of provinces in foreign policy. A concluding section is devoted to the foreign policy review of 1968–70.

Clarkson, Stephen. *Canada and the Reagan Challenge: Crisis and Adjustment, 1981–85.* Toronto: James Lorimer & Co., 1985.

This is a detailed study of Canadian/American relations during a period which included intense conflict and related negotiations over the National Energy Program and the Foreign Investment Review Agency in particular. Other topics include the Alaska Pipeline and acid rain.

---

*Those not contained in the bibliography were not included in the External Affairs documentation series and are therefore available *only* from the Public Archives of Canada. There is a parallel and equally valuable collection of statements in French on Canadian foreign policy during the Trudeau era.

Lyon, Peyton V., and Tomlin, Brian W. *Canada as an International Actor.* Toronto: Macmillan, 1979.

This book probes the foundations of Canadian behaviour in international affairs. In several ways, it is an extended discussion of the ideas and directions contained in *Foreign Policy for Canadians*, the 1968–70 foreign policy review. The authors make extensive use of polling data and of more specific articles in the field, and assess various statistical indicators of Canada's international position. They conclude: "We are left with a major mystery. Why, when all our indices locate Canada among the major powers of the international system, do a large majority of observers persist in perceiving it as a 'middle power'...?" They attribute this perception or misperception to history (i.e., Canada is still evolving and maturing), and to geography (i.e., next to the United States, Canada is small). They argue nonetheless that "Canada should now be regarded as a major power."

The authors devote extensive space to Canada's image as a nation, Canada-U.S. integration, Canada and the Third World, and Canada as a member of international organizations.

The book concludes with a critical assessment of Canada's international performance and its relationship to Canadian unity.

Martin, Laurence. *The Presidents and the Prime Ministers.* Toronto: Doubleday Canada Ltd., 1982.

This book reviews and assesses the relationships between Canadian prime ministers and United States presidents between 1867 and 1982. It devotes roughly a chapter to such twosomes as Theodore Roosevelt and Wilfrid Laurier, Mackenzie King and Franklin Roosevelt, and ends with three chapters on the Trudeau era, covering relations with five presidents. Martin believes that Mr. Trudeau's attitude to the United States was

> that of a distant pragmatist. He understood and was sensitive to the overwhelming power of the neighbour and appreciated the restrictions it placed on his elbow room. But it was imperative for him that the Canadian sense of identity endure, and if possible, strengthen....It was Trudeau's misfortune to face a streak of incompatibles and near incompatibles [among U.S. Presidents] — (LBJ, Nixon, Ford, Carter and Reagan).

Nevertheless, Martin believes Trudeau was professional and formal in his dealings with U.S. presidents, and did not allow personality differences to interfere in a businesslike relationship.

While Martin's introductory chapter is a highly readable overall statement of how president/prime minister relationships evolved over the years, until talk of a "special relationship" ended in 1972, the book is a journalistic rather than an academic treatment of the subject.

Nossal, Kim Richard. *An Acceptance of Paradox: Essays on Canadian Diplomacy in Honour of John W. Holmes.* Toronto: Canadian Institute of International Affairs, 1982.

As the title indicates, this is a book dedicated to a man who has practised, written, and taught extensively in the field of Canadian diplomacy. Most articles deal with subjects of the 1950s and 1960s when Holmes was in the public service or head of the Canadian Institute for International Affairs. However, there is an article about "Trudeau at Singapore: The Commonwealth and Arms Sales to South Africa." As well, the essay on "Canada and the Test-Ban Negotiations 1955–71" ends in the Trudeau era.

Nossal, Kim Richard. *The Politics of Canadian Foreign Policy.* Scarborough, Ontario: Prentice-Hall Canada, 1985.

This is essentially a basic political science text about how Canadian foreign policy is made. It reviews external factors in foreign policy, how Canadian society shapes foreign policy, the roles of political executives, bureaucracy, legislatures, and provincial governments. It does not address the Trudeau period per se, except that most recent foreign policy machinery was the creation of his governments. There is a brief section focused on Mr. Trudeau's approach to foreign policy.

Thomson, D.C., and Swanson, R.F. *Canadian Foreign Policy: Options and Perspectives.* Toronto: McGraw-Hill Ryerson, 1971.

This book is not so much about foreign policy in the Trudeau era as about the conditions and factors which led to the foreign policy review of 1968–70. It begins with a description and assessment of that review and notes that it did not "provide all of the elements necessary to the understanding of Canadian foreign policy in the 1970s, particularly for readers unfamiliar with the subject." The authors try to fill these gaps from a lay reader's perspective, addressing historical evolution, Canada and Europe, East-West tensions, Third World relations, the Pacific rim, and the Canada-U.S. relationship.

Thordarson, Bruce. *Trudeau and Foreign Policy: A Study in Decision-Making.* Toronto: Oxford University Press, 1972.

This is a detailed examination of the foreign policy review conducted between May 1968 and June 1970. It examines the different factors at work in formulating a new foreign policy, including the Prime Minister's views on *how* policy should be made. The author concludes that, despite its comprehensive style, the review was not a radical departure from the past and omitted key international issues and relationships, though it did result in a number of changes in the *emphasis* of foreign policy.

Tomlin, Brian W., ed. *Canada's Foreign Policy: Analysis and Trends.* Toronto: Methuen, 1978.

This book is geared to creation of "middle-range theories" about how Canadian foreign policy is developed and conducted. It resulted from efforts of the Inter-University Seminar on International Relations. Each of its three parts contains an article on the "Third Option," namely the development of counterweights to American influence on Canada, and adoption of a more independent foreign policy. Among these is an innovative survey of expert opinion (called a "Delphi forecast") on the likelihood of success of the Third Option. The weight of opinion is pessimistic about such a possibility.

Tomlin, Brian W., and Molot, Maureen, eds. *Canada among Nations — 1984: A Time of Transition.* Toronto: Lorimer & Co., 1985.

This book contains ten articles reviewing different aspects of Canadian international relations in 1984, ranging from the world economy, to development assistance policy, to "managing Canadian foreign policy." The book concludes with a chronology of events and a statistical profile of the year.

Although several articles touch on the efforts of the Trudeau government, two in particular are helpful on this subject. John Kirton's chapter on "Managing Canadian Foreign Policy" contains a useful four-page summary of the Trudeau legacy in foreign affairs, as a prelude to discussion of what his successors would do. Kirton pays particular attention to how Mr. Trudeau reshaped foreign policy-making apparatus in Canada. Harold van Riekhoff and John Sigler have written an extensive critical evaluation of the Trudeau "peace initiative" of 1983–84 which draws on the press and periodical articles written in its wake. After reviewing the various critiques others had written and examining the initiative themselves, they conclude that it "had been a difficult and daring undertaking and, at best only a partial success."

Tucker, Michael. *Canadian Foreign Policy: Contemporary Issues and Themes.* Toronto: McGraw-Hill Ryerson, 1980.

This book is probably the most detailed and extensive treatment of the Trudeau Government's foreign policy and international relations between 1968 and 1979. Tucker's overall theme is that, despite Mr. Trudeau's desire to create a "national foreign policy for Canada which would break from the past in significant ways, the actual practice of foreign affairs went on much as it had in the past." Tucker notes that Mr. Trudeau's concept of a foreign policy which would serve Canada's "national interests" was specific to him. "Trudeau's nationalism was in its essence a form of internationalism . . . He conceived of Canada as a mentor state, taking initiatives on behalf of the world community." In fact, Tucker considers that with "his belief in Canada's right and responsibility to help reduce global tensions, Pierre Trudeau was a Pearsonian. . . .[He] felt, as did Pearson, that Canadian interests and values could often best be expressed through international relationships." Other topics covered in the book include domestic sources of foreign policy, the Canadian-American relationship, the United Nations, the European Economic Community, defence policy, the law of the sea, and non-proliferation of nuclear weapons.

B: RELEVANT PUBLISHED WORKS OF PIERRE ELLIOTT TRUDEAU

"A Canadian leader looks at the Soviet Union." Ottawa, May 28, 1971. *Statements and Speeches,* 71/16

"A Canadian view of the Commonwealth." Ottawa, January 5, 1971. *Statements and Speeches,* 71/1

"A Defence Policy for Canada." *External Affairs,* XXI (May 1969), 214–15

"Address, 23 January 1976, Mexico City." Ottawa: Office of the Prime Minister, 1976 (press release)

"Address, 28 January 1976, Cienfuegos, Cuba." Ottawa: Office of the Prime Minister, 1976 (press release)

"Address, 30 January 1976, Caracas, Venezuela." Ottawa: Office of the Prime Minister, 1976 (press release)

"Address: Canadian and American friendship: Canada's unity will not be fractured." Delivered to the Congress of the United States, February 22, 1977. *Vital Speeches of the Day*, 43 (March 15, 1977) 322-24

"Address to CALA V conference, January 31, 1976, Caracas, Venezuela." Ottawa: Office of the Prime Minister, 1976 (press release)

"Address to the General Assembly of the United Nations Special Session on Disarmament," May 26, 1978. Ottawa: Office of the Prime Minister (press release)

"A global initiative to improve the prospects for peace" Montreal, November 13, 1983. *Statements and Speeches*, 83/20

"Call for more solid links between France and Canada," Paris, November 9, 1982. *Statements and Speeches*, 82/31

"Canada and China: a little mutual education." Peking, October 13, 1973. *Statements and Speeches*, 73/20

"Canada and La Francophonie." Paris, November 10, 1982. *Statements and Speeches*, 82/32

"Canada and Nigeria share a common culture." *External Affairs,* XXI (November 1969) 399-402

"Canada and the European Economic Community." Ottawa, October 28, 1974. *Statements and Speeches*, 74/12

"Canada and the Pacific." *Far Eastern Economic Review*, LXXIV (December 18, 1971) 27

"Canada and the world." *External Affairs*, XX (July 1968) 278-84

"Canada assesses the new U.S. economic measures." *External Affairs*, XXIII (September 1971) 326-27

"Canada leads the fight against pollution." Toronto, April 15, 1970. *Statements and Speeches*, 70/3

"Canada's obligations as a nuclear power." Ottawa, June 17, 1975. *Statements and Speeches*, 75/22

"Canada's position on testing Cruise missiles and on disarmament," Ottawa, May 9, 1983. *Statements and Speeches*, 83/8

"Charter of the United Nations: its twenty-fifth anniversary." Statement in the House of Commons, June 26, 1970. *External Affairs* XXII (September 1970) 311-12

"Commonwealth Conference." Report to the House of Commons, January 20, 1969. *External Affairs* XXI (February 1969) 102-5

"Commonwealth meetings: their special character." Ottawa, August 10, 1973. *Statements and Speeches*, 73/26

Conversations with Canadians. Toronto: University of Toronto Press, 1972.

"Defence policy and foreign policy." Speech to the Alberta Liberal Association, April 12, 1969. *External Affairs*, XXI (June 1969) 249-56

Deux Innocents en Chine rouge. Montréal: Éditions de l'Homme, 1961 (avec Jaques Hébert)

"Double Allégeance du Canada: Francophonie et la Commonwealth." Hiver 1978/9, *Politique internationale*, no. 2, 33-42

"Freedom and democracy: the strength and problem of NATO." Brussels, May 30, 1975. *Statements and Speeches*, 84/2.

"Initiatives for peace and security." Ottawa, February 9, 1984. *Statements and Speeches*, 75/19

"International development as a requisite for peace." *External Affairs*, XX (June 1968) 246–50

"Need for the renewal of a disciplined and compassionate world order." Ottawa, May 6, 1983. *Statements and Speeches*, 83/7

"New Canadian ties with China." Ottawa, October 19, 1973. *Statements and Speeches*, 73/20

"New and renewable energy sources: the need and a response." Nairobi, August 11, 1981. *Statements and Speeches* 81/22

"Prime Minister looks at China [excerpts from statements made October 13 during Trudeau's visit to China, and to the House of Commons, October 19, 1973]." *International Perspectives* (January/February 1974), 10–11

"Prime Minister Trudeau talks to the Soviet leaders May 17 to 28, 1971." Ottawa, May 28, 1971. *Statements and Speeches*, 71/17

"Reflections on peace and security," Guelph, Ontario, October 27, 1983. *Statements and Speeches*, 83/18

"Rekindling 'the spirit of Ottawa'." Ottawa, September 25, 1974. *Statements and Speeches*, 74/14

"Statement at the NATO summit, Washington, D.C., May 30, 1978." Ottawa: Office of the Prime Minister (press release)

"Technological momentum: the fuel that feeds the nuclear arms race," New York, June 10, 1982. *Statements and Speeches* 82/10

"The Commonwealth after Ottawa." *The Round Table*, no. 253 (January 1974), 35–42

"The Commonwealth: an association unstructured and unfettered." Ottawa, August 2, 1973. *Statements and Speeches*, 73/25

"The Commonwealth in the seventies." Singapore, January 21, 1971. *Statements and Speeches*, 71/4

"The Commonwealth heads of government meeting." Singapore — I, February 1, 1971. *Statements and Speeches*, 71/5

"The Commonwealth heads of government meeting." Singapore — I, February 2, 1971. *Statements and Speeches*, 71/6

"The compelling need for progress in North/South relations," House of Commons, June 15, 1981. *Statements and Speeches* 81/17

"The conflict in Nigeria." Statement to the House on November 26, 1968. December 1968, *External Affairs*, XX, 486–95

"The contractual link: a Canadian contribution to the vocabulary of co-operation." London, March 15, 1975. *Statements and Speeches*, 75/6

"The lessons of Helsinki," Helsinki, July 30, 1975. *Statements and Speeches*, 75/24

"The Nigerian situation." House of Commons, November 26, 1968. *Statements and Speeches*, 68/19

"The problem of relief for secessionist Nigeria — I." House of Commons, November 25, 1969. *Statements and Speeches*, 69/21

"The problem of relief for secessionist Nigeria — II." House of Commons, November 27, 1969. *Statements and Speeches*, 69/22

"The relation of defence policy to foreign policy." Calgary, April 12, 1969. *Statements and Speeches*, 69/8

"The road to economic recovery." Spring, 1978, *Atlantic Community Quarterly*, 16, 139-49 (speech presented to the Economic Club of New York, 22 March 1978)

"The situation in Southern Africa." Singapore, January 20, 1971. *Statements and Speeches*, 71/3

"The role of the Commonwealth." House of Commons, January 20, 1969. *Statements and Speeches*, 69/5

"Tied aid or not?" *Ceres I* (September-October 1968), 14

"Transcript of press conference, Ottawa, 14 December 1978." Ottawa: Office of the Prime Minister, 1978 (press release)

Two innocents in Red China, tr. by I.M. Owen. Toronto: Oxford, 1968 (with Jacques Hébert)

"U.N. Day: a time for rededication." *External Affairs*, XX (November 1968) 456-57

"White House joint statement, 8 September 1977." Ottawa: United States Information Service (press release 77-3)

C: BIBLIOGRAPHIES OF MATERIALS COVERING THE TRUDEAU ERA IN FOREIGN POLICY

Barrett, Jane R., & Beaumont, Jane. *A Bibliography of Works on Canadian Foreign Relations, 1976-1980*. Toronto: Canadian Institute of International Affairs, 1982.

Donneur, André. *Politique étrangère du Canada: bibliographie 1972-1975*. Montréal: Département de Science politique, Université du Québec à Montréal, 1976.

—. *Politique étrangère du Canada: bibliographie 1976-1977*. Montreal: Département de Science politique, Université du Québec à Montréal, 1978.

Motiuk, Laurence, & Grant, Madeline. *A Reading Guide to Canada in World Affairs*. Toronto: Canadian Institute of International Affairs, 1972.

Page, Donald M. *A Bibliography of Works on Canadian Foreign Relations, 1945-1970*. Toronto: Canadian Institute of International Affairs, 1973.

—. *A Bibliography of Works on Canadian Foreign Relations, 1971-1975*. Toronto: Canadian Institute of International Affairs, 1977.

Smith, Dwight L. *The History of Canada: An Annotated Bibliography*. Santa Barbara, CA: American Bibliographical Center, Clio Press, 1983.

Biography

The Right Honourable Pierre Elliott Trudeau, P.C., C.C., C.H., Q.C., M.A., LL.L., LL.D., M.R.S.C.

*P*ierre Elliott Trudeau was born in Montreal, Quebec, on October 18, 1919, the son of Charles-Émile Trudeau and Grace Elliott. He was educated in public schools and collegiate institutes in Montreal. In 1940, he graduated from Jean de Brébeuf College, Montreal, with a B.A., Honours standing. Then he studied law at the University of Montreal, graduating with Honours in 1943. He received his M.A. in political economy from Harvard University in 1945. There followed several years of post-graduate studies in law, economics, and political science at the École des sciences politiques in Paris and the London School of Economics. Mr. Trudeau was called to the bar of the Province of Quebec in 1943.

In 1949, he joined the Privy Council Office in Ottawa as a desk officer. Beginning in 1951, he practised law, specializing in labour law and civil liberties cases in the Province of Quebec; at the same time, he co-founded and co-directed the monthly publication of a review entitled *Cité Libre*. In 1961, he was appointed Associate Professor of Law, University of Montreal. He taught constitutional law and civil liberties and carried out research while on the staff of the Institut de recherches en droit public.

In 1965, he was elected as a Liberal to the House of Commons for the constituency of Mount Royal. He was appointed Parliamentary Secretary to Prime Minister Lester B. Pearson in January 1966, and was reappointed to this post in January 1967. Mr. Trudeau became Minister of Justice and Attorney General of Canada on April 4, 1967. Following the announcement of Mr. Pearson's retirement, Mr. Trudeau was elected Leader of the Liberal Party of Canada at a leadership convention in Ottawa on April 6, 1968. He was sworn in as Prime Minister of Canada on April 20, 1968. Following the defeat of the Liberal party in the general election of May 22, 1979, he resigned as Prime Minister on June 4. He became Leader of the Official Opposition during the period of the Progressive Conservative Government of the Right Honourable Joe Clark, which was defeated in a House of Commons vote on December 13, 1979.

Mr. Trudeau was sworn in as Prime Minister of Canada again on March 3,

1980, following the general election of February 18, 1980. Mr. Trudeau was elected Member of Parliament for Mount Royal in the general election of June 25, 1968. He was re-elected on October 30, 1972, July 8, 1974, May 22, 1979, and February 18, 1980.

Honorary degrees and awards Mr. Trudeau has received over the years include: Doctorate of Laws, University of Alberta, 1968; Queen's University, 1968; Doctorate of Letters, University of Moncton, 1969; Doctorate of Laws, University of Ottawa, 1974, Duke University, 1974; Order of Merit, University of Montreal, 1975; Freeman of the City of London, 1975; Dean of the Faculty of Law, University of Poitiers, 1975; Doctorate of Laws, University of Tokyo, 1976; Berkeley Citation, University of California, 1977; Family of Man Award, New York City Council of Churches, 1981; Doctorate of Laws, St. Francis Xavier University, 1982; Notre Dame University, 1982; Doctorate of Laws, Dalhousie University, 1983; Albert Einstein Peace Prize, 1984; Companion of the Order of Canada, November 1985.

He was previously married to Margaret Joan Sinclair and has three children (Justin Pierre, Alexandre Emmanuel, and Michel Charles-Émile).

Index